Aglow
Lorraine Mitchell

Lost in the
MONEY
MAZE?

How to
Find Your
Way
Through

PATRICIA H. RUSHFORD

D1115503

Aglow Publications

A Ministry of Women's Aglow Fellowship, Int'l.
P.O. Box 1548
Lynnwood, WA 98046-1548
USA

Cover design by David Marty

Women's Aglow Fellowship, Int'l. is a non-denominational organization of Christian women. Our mission is to provide support, education, training, and ministry opportunities to help women worldwide discover their true identity in Jesus Christ through the power of the Holy Spirit.

Aglow Publications is the publishing ministry of Women's Aglow Fellowship, Int'l. Our publications are used to help women find a personal relationship with Jesus Christ, to enhance growth in their Christian experience, and to help them recognize their roles and relationship according to scripture.

For more information about Women's Aglow Fellowship, please write to Women's Aglow Fellowship, Int'l., P.O. Box 1548, Lynnwood, WA 98046-1548, USA or call (206) 775-7282.

Unless otherwise noted, all scripture quotations in this publication are from the Holy Bible, New International Version. Copyright 1973, 1978, 1984, International Bible Society. Other versions are abbreviated as follows: TLB (The Living Bible), RSV (Revised Standard Version).

ISBN 0-932305-91-1

Acknowledgments

Special thanks to Gloria Chisholm, my editor and friend; my husband, Ron; Margo Power; Cleta Chrisman; Jeff and Micki Knight; Sally Kaufman; and Sharon Bumala for their guidance, expertise, wisdom, and support.

Contents

Contents

Foreword

Financial experts tell us that only one-third of Americans are doing okay in handling their money. One-third are barely surviving, just managing to stay solvent. And one-third are in deep financial trouble—they are complete failures at money management.

My own experience is that at least two-thirds of all folks have real trouble balancing earning, giving, spending, and saving their money.

Christian authors and publishers have responded to this obvious need for financial help with an abundance of books and seminars on biblical money management. Having read most of these books and attended many seminars, I've wondered what else needed to be written on this subject.

From the moment I started Pat Rushford's book, I was hooked by her creative, fun language. Her descriptions of women's battles, the tantalizing spending temptations of busy mothers, and the special financial pressures of working women made it obvious that this author has lived in the household maze where women live.

Whether single, married, divorced, or widowed, whether employed outside the home or busy as a full-time homemaker, women will find this book has sound advice and practical ideas.

I've often sensed that most of us who wrote and taught biblical principles were men who really did leave a gap in the kinds of information needed by women. *Lost in the Money Maze? How to Find Your Way Through* fills that gap.

Lots of products are touted with the claim that they don't cost—they pay. Anyone reading this book can easily save its cost by putting into practice, for one week, any one of the many excellent ideas offered here.

Lost in the Money Maze?

Although this book was written for women, I enjoyed it thoroughly. It is the kind of light reading that could help most men understand the different financial roles of their wives and daughters.

We've all heard that most of us don't use our God-given creativity very well. Every chapter of this book stimulated my creativity. If it does that for every reader, and in the process makes the stewardship of your money and possessions more pleasing to God, then Pat Rushford will have succeeded in her purpose.

George Fooshee, author
You Can Beat the Money Squeeze

Introduction

In the beginning, God placed humankind in charge of the whole earth. We've come a long way since the beginning and, in some ways, we have not only managed to subdue the earth, but to abuse much of it. There is one area, however, where most of us consistently fail to achieve control, and that is in the area of handling money.

Money in itself is powerless, but all too often human greed grants it the power to destroy and corrupt. At the same time, under the influence of human love, money can work for us. It can be a blessing, a God-given abundance, a gift that God gives his children for their pleasure and good work. Yet, for all too many Christians, money has mutated from kindly servant to unleashed monster—it has become a brutal taskmaster to which millions consistently bow.

Lost in the Money Maze? How to Find Your Way Through is dedicated to those who are caught in an endless maze of earning, spending, balancing, and saving money. Although this book is loaded with basic money management techniques, we'll also examine our relationship with money, our desire for it, the loving and hating of it, where and why it disappears so quickly, how difficult it is to manage, and how money matters fit into our spiritual lives. We'll also discuss the psychology of spending, the highs and the lows, the guilt and fears surrounding the subject of money. And, perhaps most importantly, we'll look at some biblical principles that can help us discern God's will for the financial picture in our lives.

Lost in the Money Maze? How to Find Your Way Through is written for those of us who care about money matters and wonder how our financial responsibilities relate to God's will. It offers money saving and budgeting advice, plus a variety of bookkeeping methods designed to fit your personality. Most importantly, it offers a plan that will enable you to escape your money maze.

Like many people, maybe you'd rather tame rattle-snakes than read about money, but perhaps the Holy Spirit has nudged you, and you know in your heart that this is an area of your life that needs attention. The dark side of money must be exposed to the light and examined so that the Holy Spirit can reveal God's will to you and help you move closer to a fruitful, spirit-filled, and holy life.

Part I
The Money Maze

"Money is like an unfaithful spouse, it runs out on you."

"Every time I think about doing taxes I break out in a cold sweat."

"Paying bills puts me in a slump for a week. I have to go out and buy something to relieve the depression."

"The last time my checkbook balanced was when I opened the account."

"Money is magic—it disappears."

Sound familiar? These sentiments toward money may or may not necessarily be yours, but I have a hunch, if you're wandering—or stumbling—through a maze of financial responsibilities, you can easily add your own caustic one-liners to the collection. Perhaps you, like most people these days, find your financial journey anything but delightful. You long for financial freedom, but you just can't find your way through the labyrinth of ever-increasing debts. This is a book about money and how to use it, instead of letting it use you. As we work through the money maze, we'll discover ways to move beyond the oppressive obstacles of too many bills, not enough money, and mounting debts into a realm of financial and emotional stability and freedom.

The first step in finding a way through the money maze is to examine our attitudes and feelings toward money and the level of our commitment to find solutions. Then we scrutinize our abilities as money managers and address specific problem areas. Finally, we discover and implement specific techniques to help us resolve our money problems and the emotional turmoil they can bring.

To begin our journey into financial freedom, let's move on to chapter 1 and meet a reluctant sojourner who'd rather not have anything to do with money matters.

1
...

Confessions of a Financial Failure

It happened again. The preacher's words pierced Janet's heart like nails. He repeated the all too familiar verse and hammered the message deeper. "'No one can serve two masters. Either he will hate the one and love the other, or he will be devoted to the one and despise the other. You cannot serve both God and Money.'"[1] He raised his voice and delivered another blow. "The Bible says, '. . . a man is a slave to whatever has mastered him.'[2] Now I ask you . . . do you control your money? Or are you a slave to money and what it can buy?"

Janet tried to tune out the pastor's hard-hitting words and the feelings he evoked. She hated sermons on money.

She had often prayed that God would free her and Rob from their debts. But nothing changed. If anything, their money problems were getting worse. She hated feeling guilty. After all, it wasn't her fault. Janet had even taken a job to help out and they still couldn't get ahead. She looked down at one of the reasons. The tiny bundle nestled in her arms, Sarah, had cost them more than six thousand dollars in medical bills. Rob had switched jobs and the new insurance wouldn't cover the pregnancy. If everything went all right, Sarah would be paid for by the time she was ready for college.

"We are called to serve God!" the pastor's voice boomed over the loudspeaker. Janet jumped; Sarah let out a wail. Janet breathed a sigh of relief. She would have to take the baby out of the service. With any luck it would take twenty minutes to calm little Sarah down, and Janet would miss the rest of the sermon. But Sarah greedily accepted the nipple Janet thrust into her mouth and drifted off to sleep. And Janet was forced to sit and listen to more of the condemning message.

Why couldn't the pastor have chosen another topic, like "blessed are the poor"? Of course it didn't help that Rob had gone out shopping the day before and purchased a hot tub. She had objected at first but . . . it was on sale . . . and after a hard day's work their muscles ached, and they had to have *some* fun didn't they? What good is money if you can't enjoy it? After all, they hardly ever spent money for recreation. And it wasn't as though they couldn't afford it. They'd just paid off their furniture bill so they'd only be paying an extra sixty dollars a month. And Rob's new job would eventually bring in more income.

As the pastor droned on Janet imagined her family wandering through a money maze. Like prisoners they were trapped in a maze with nothing but dead ends. The only thing that seemed to keep the paths open was to try to make more money.

Janet wanted desperately to break the barriers and walk

away because she knew that the real controlling influence in her life was not the Holy Spirit, but this big, inescapable dictator labeled Money.

She swallowed the massive lump of guilt in her throat and wished she had stayed home from church. This was an area of her life from which she wanted to escape, but it was too overwhelming, too powerful to fight. The best she could hope for was enough strength to cover up her fears, ignore the problems, and maybe keep looking for a way out.

Janet tried to push the troublesome image of the money maze from her mind. Luckily, her two-year-old son, Kevin, chose that moment to tear pages out of the hymnal and she quickly—and thankfully—diverted her attention from her money problems to the timely task at hand.

THE PROBLEM WITH MONEY

Are Janet's and Rob's struggles only too familiar to you? Many of us wrestle daily with financial difficulties. They, like millions of others, are dealing with serious money problems and, in this and the following chapter, we'll look at these in more depth. They are:

- A desire to run away from financial difficulties.
- The need to make excuses for poor money management.
- The tendency to spend money before it's earned.
- A habit of unhealthy spending.
- The feeling of being trapped by indebtedness.
- Confusion about the role money is to play in our lives.
- The lack of team effort between husband and wife.
- The tendency to ignore feelings of guilt.
- The lack of budgeting and bookkeeping skills.
- A lack of financial facts.

Now let's take a closer look at a few of these difficulties.

Lost in the Money Maze?

As we do, consider how these issues may be at work in your own life.

Janet tried to ignore her financial responsibilities and made excuses for her lack of involvement. You may consider her foolish; on the other hand, you may understand her motives only too well.

"I Don't Have Time to Manage Money"

Many women echo Janet's lament: "I don't have time to manage money. By the time I manage my kids, the house, my husband, my job, the dog, the cat, and the gerbils, I have barely enough energy left to manage myself."

Life is hard. With all of our responsibilities, the last thing we need is to worry about debts, budgets, taxes, or investments. My friend Ellen never had time for money management until her forty-two-year-old husband, Barney, left her. She never expected divorce to soil their "blissful" marriage. He was always so solid and committed—certainly not the type to have an affair and leave his wife after twenty years.

In the divorce settlement, she got a four-bedroom Victorian house, three kids, a dog, a hamster, and a canary— all either hungry or in need of repair. She was thankful for a place to live, but as Ellen said, "What good is a house when you can't afford the upkeep and the payments?"

Ellen felt she had no skills or means of securing a job or money. "I never paid much attention to our financial dealings," she confessed. "All I ever did was manage a small allowance that Barney gave me. I couldn't even balance a checkbook."

Fortunately, Ellen's story doesn't end there. Through a county assistance program, Ellen received monthly allowances and the opportunity to attend a community college for job training. She also learned some basic record-keeping and budgeting skills. Today, Ellen manages her own restaurant business. "Every woman," Ellen says, "should have the good sense to at least know the basics of money management."

"It's My Husband's Responsibility . . . Isn't It?"

Even today, when most women cringe at a sexist remark like that, a few women are all too eager to let hubby handle the finances. A recent newspaper article stated, "Despite the number of women in the work place, professional investors say many [women] have no say in how the family's money is invested."[3]

Many women I've talked with have told me they had no intention of getting involved in financial affairs.

Victoria, for example, winked and said, "Manage money? Me? No thanks. I'll leave that mess to Joe. Besides. . . ." She grinned. "Making money is his job. Mine is to spend it."

Sally, thirty-three and married with 2.4 children, told me firmly, "I feel that it's up to the husband to manage the money. The Bible says the man should be the head of the home. And frankly, he can have it. I don't need the hassle."

A number of women, however, might hear Sally's and Victoria's remarks and shake their heads. They have learned the hard way that naiveté toward financial responsibilities is an indulgence few women can afford.

While spending the money their husbands earn and enjoying financial freedom without restrictions and responsibilities of management may seem like great sport, women who don't get involved in financial responsibilities are not being realistic. After all, what happens if their husbands are no longer on the scene to play the role as the family's sole supporter?

That won't happen? Let's hope not, but before you turn

17

down a financial education, look at these facts.

• Women tend to live longer than men. Statistics tell us that we will probably outlive our husbands. Consequently, we'd better prepare ourselves to step into the role of breadwinner as well as money manager.

• Divorce. We have only to take a look at the lives of those around us to see the reality of how often divorce fractures families. You may be saying, "Yes, but I don't believe in divorce," or "It will never happen to us." Unfortunately, divorce can and does happen—often to those who least expect it.

• The total percentage of American women who work has escalated from about forty-three percent in 1970 to about seventy percent today. While many women choose to pursue careers, many others, in trying to stay solvent financially, are compelled to take full- or part-time jobs.

The days of dependence on men to provide financial support, maintain the budget, and function as the family's money manager are over. Venita VanCaspel, in her book *The Power of Money Dynamics*, admonishes women who shirk their financial responsibilities. "If you are a woman," Venita warns, "don't ever think it is your inalienable right that a man should take care of your financial security. The single state—whether through choice, circumstances, death or divorce—will probably be your lot for at least a part or all of your life. Even if you marry, you have an obligation to be a financial partner to your husband and to be as well informed as you can about money."[4]

Getting to know about money matters is not only for women who don't have partners. A wise woman will insist on sharing the family financial responsibilities with her husband. In some cases, when the husband isn't a good money manager, she may have to take the lead. But either way, managing money should be a team effort that involves the whole family.

As to Sally's remark about using the Bible as an excuse to hand money management over to the "man of the house," I encouraged her to take another look at what scripture really does say on the matter.

Somewhere along the line, certain religious groups have gotten the notion that it isn't biblical for wives to manage financial affairs. It follows the adage, *a woman's place is in the home*. Because of varying religious views on the roles women supposedly *should* take, I'd like to focus, for a moment, on an influential woman who lived back in about 400 B.C.

If scripture has determined that women are to steer clear of managing money, households, or anything else, then the "virtuous woman" of Proverbs 31 and the man who praised her were unabashedly living in sin. Yet the Bible tells us ". . . she is worth far more than rubies!" She was trustworthy, helpful, generous, and able to meet her husband's needs. Not only that, her financial endeavors were unlimited. She managed a household, invested in real estate, owned a vineyard, owned and operated her own garment industry, and on the whole seemed financially secure. The evidence suggests she was wealthy— she wore purple and had servant girls. Yet, rather than store up treasures with her Nordstrom's and Sak's Fifth Avenue credit cards, she hunted for bargains, made clothes for her family and herself, and gave generously to the poor. "She is clothed with strength and dignity . . . she speaks with wisdom, and faithful instruction is on her tongue."[5]

Most women would find it difficult to wear her tunic, and some wouldn't even want to try. I didn't bring this virtuous woman into the picture to dump a load of guilt on you. I simply wanted to show that women can take an active part in money management without selling their souls. Finding a way through the money maze is as much a woman's job as it is a man's. We'll talk more about sharing responsibilities later, but for now, let's move on to another, and perhaps more common money problem.

"It's Not My Fault"

"We had to declare bankruptcy. There was no other way. We just had too many bills. We needed that new car. Everybody uses credit these days. Taxes are too high. It's John's fault . . . he has this reward mentality. These $175 tennis shoes were the only ones my son would wear. Kids need brand-name clothes in order to be accepted by their peers. If I got paid what I'm worth we wouldn't have a problem. I have a big deal coming in next week."

Ever since Eve talked Adam into eating the forbidden fruit, people have been blaming others for their problems and indiscretions. We blame the system, the government, the institutions; we blame husbands and wives, children, and sometimes we even blame God.

We confuse our needs and wants and refuse to face the fact that, in all probability, we are at least partially, if not fully, responsible for our financial situation. Of course, we do sometimes experience medical emergencies and natural disasters over which we have no control, but, for the most part, our misadventures in the money maze were forged by our own lack of discipline, poor management skills, immaturity, and lack of understanding. One of the major difficulties in assessing our attitudes is confusion about the role money is to play in our lives.

TWO SIDES OF THE COIN

The Bible seems to take two sides on the money issue. In some instances, money is referred to as a blessing—as

God's reward for faithfulness to him.[6] We are told not to worry, that if we seek God first, all our needs will be met.[7] We're told that if we give, we will receive.[8] We see that money can be used to feed the hungry, clothe the poor, and nurse the sick—these are all good things. Jesus seemed to enjoy certain aspects of wealth. He ate with wealthy men and tax collectors like Zacchaeus and with Pharisees.[9] When a woman anointed him with expensive perfume, he praised her and chided his disciples for their criticism of what they saw as wastefulness.[10]

Yet, in other Bible passages, Jesus seems to contradict the idea of blessings and abundance and sharply criticizes the wealthy. "But woe to you who are rich . . ."[11] He tells us what a terrible trap money is and that it's easier for a camel to go through a needle's eye than for a rich person to enter heaven.[12] In fact he even says, ". . . any of you who does not give up everything he [she] has cannot be my disciple."[13]

So we find ourselves in a bind where money is concerned. In our society, we can't exist without it, yet if we have too much of it, we may get into trouble spiritually. At times I wonder if this confusion regarding riches might contribute to some people's spending habits. Some may subconsciously think, *If I stay in debt, I'll be too poor to worry about being too rich. Because being rich might keep me out of heaven.* In actuality, of course, it is our heart attitude toward money, not the lack or abundance of it that gets us into trouble spiritually.

Deep inside a great and powerful fear may prevent us from looking too deeply into Christ's teaching on money. Richard Foster, in his book *Money, Sex and Power*, says:

The most difficult thing we have to deal with when we begin to look at the dark side of money is fear. If we have any sense at all, these words of Jesus really do frighten us.[14]

If we look too deep, we may find that we have been stained and dirtied by affluence. We may be challenged to give up all that we have and to simplify our life styles. We may come face to face with a terrible and ugly dark side of ourselves called greed, lust, and hunger for the power money can bring.

In our confusion and fear, we may find it easier to keep busy, make excuses, spend more money, do *anything* that keeps us from examining that distasteful element in our lives and coming face-to-face with money's influence and how it hinders our relationship with God. In fact, many find it easier to talk about the secrets of their sex life than about their money affairs. Instead of carefully weighing the facts and studying God's will and Christ's meaning, we choose to ignore the issues, and thus sidestep whatever pain and discomfort the truth might bring.

But do we really have a choice? Since our attitudes toward money, our level of financial awareness, and our involvement in money matters directly reflects our relationship to God, do we dare ignore the problem?

If we desire to come to God completely, and if we are to fulfill that desire, we'll want to expose the dark and dusty corners—the obstacles and dead ends of our money maze. We need a thorough, honest investigation and evaluation of what that maze contains. Then and only then can we discover the right path that will lead us to financial freedom.

In this first chapter, we've brought to light some of our excuses, fears, and confusion regarding money matters. In a few minutes, we'll head into chapter 2 where we'll test our financial aptitudes. But first, let's take some time to think about our attitudes. Whether we have money or not, whether we manage it or not, we'll want to examine the money maze in which we find ourselves.

Ask God to shine a light on the dark alleys and guide you through. Ask him to help you view your attitudes toward money from his perspective. I hope at this point you are ready to accept the challenge to examine the obstacles in your money maze more closely. Below you'll find some exercises to help you do that.

TIME TO CONSIDER

1. To place God first in your life is to surrender yourself completely to him. It is to follow your Lord at all costs. It is to be indebted only to him. It is to loosen your grip on all things and cling only to him. I believe it was Corrie Ten-Boom who once said, "I have learned not to hold too tightly to things because it hurts too much when God makes me let go." How much of your life is totally surrendered to God? Be specific.

2. Use a notebook or diary to write down any fears, questions, prayers, and answers that may come to you. You may want to work with a spouse, friend, or support group so that you can encourage one another and share concerns and confess wrong actions, thoughts, and attitudes. (If you form a support group it is important to maintain confidentiality.)

3. How tightly are you holding on to your job, your home, your clothing, your charge cards? I'm not going to ask you to give up all you own—only God has that right— but it *is* important to get in touch with the way we really feel about what we have. Then, we can work with God to correct the errors we find. In your notebook, make a list of the things you hold tightly to. When you get to the end of

our financial journey we'll look at the list again and see if your attitudes have changed.

4. How do you feel about money management? Are you eager to forge ahead? Do you want to run and hide? Get to know your inner self, your attitudes, and your feelings—be honest with yourself, others, and God.

5. When money rules us, our spiritual fruit becomes diseased, our spirits crushed. And ironically, it is not the money itself that destroys, but our attitude toward it. The crushing truth is that we have no one to blame but ourselves, and the only way out is through change.

Change is perhaps the most difficult word in the English language because it demands something from us. It hits us full force with the truth of our free will and the consequences of our actions. *Are you willing to change?*

If you desire to confront and conquer the money maze in your life, to totally surrender your financial life to God, then pray for commitment.

PRAYER

Holy Spirit, illuminate the darkness and our sinful acts, attitudes, and thoughts in the light of your truth so that we can confess them, repent of wrongdoing, and change. Help us view ourselves and our financial burdens through your eyes, so we can see with compassion and love rather than with condemnation and disgust.

Thank you, Lord, that we can come to you with our financial problems. Make us secure in the knowledge that your desire for our financial freedom is even greater than our own.

We commit ourselves to doing all that is in our power to obey your Word, to conquer our money problems, and to find the path that will lead us out of the money maze and onto the path of righteousness. Amen.

2
...
Financial Geniuses and the Rest of Us

"How about meeting me for lunch Wednesday?" I suggested to my friend Janet over coffee.

"Oh, I'd love to . . . but I can't." After a long, audible sigh, she explained. "I just paid the bills, and it looks like I've got about five dollars to last until the end of the month."

"Five dollars! But it's only the first."

"Don't I know it. I'll just have to let some of the bills go. Looks like it will be another month of casseroles, rice, and beans. I don't understand it. Rob got a raise a couple of months ago. I thought with that and my job we'd have plenty of money, but we're no better off than when I was staying home."

"Janet." I paused to swallow a bite of a poppy seed muffin. "A lot of people have trouble handling money. I don't mean to pry, but maybe you and Rob should take that financial awareness course the college is offering." I'd have offered to loan her this book, but I hadn't finished it yet.

"Oh, I don't have time for that," she said flippantly. "Besides, I'm already aware of money—acutely aware of money. In fact, I can't do without money. It just doesn't stay with me long enough to build any sort of lasting relationship."

The frantic pitch to her voice told me I'd touched an emotional nerve, and I decided not to press my point, at least for the time being. After a long couple of minutes, Janet set her coffee mug on the table.

"I'm sorry," she said as she folded her arms on the table and leaned forward. "I know you're trying to help. It's just that every time I pay the bills, I feel like every creditor is a giant with a whip standing over me, yelling, 'Pay! Pay! Pay!' I feel trapped in a maze where all the roads lead to a dead end. There's one crisis after another and they all require money. Then there's the guilt. I know God would like us to get out of debt and manage our money better, but it's hopeless."

"Janet, I've never known you to call anything hopeless. Where's the old I-can-do-anything spirit?"

"It fizzled." She frowned and took courage from another sip of coffee. "I try, you know. I really try. After taxes last year I swore I'd get our finances organized."

"Bad experience, huh?"

"The worst. You should have seen the bookkeeper's face when I showed up with *the drawer* and dumped the contents on her desk. It was so-o-o embarrassing. Anyway, I decided to buy a money book." Janet bit her bottom lip, rolled her eyes, and moaned. "After wading through three pages I threw it in the trash. It was like reading Greek!"

"Sounds like you just got the wrong book. Besides,

you're an intelligent woman. You must have learned something," I said.

"Sure," Janet teased. "I learned that if I were to rate myself from one to ten on the Financial Genius Scale, I'd weigh in at a minus three."

Of course Janet was exaggerating. If I were to score her, I'd give her at least a minus two. Inability to manage money, as I'd mentioned to Janet, is a problem millions of people share. Perhaps you can empathize with Janet or know someone who shares similar financial struggles. And possibly, even though you are reading this book, you don't relate to Janet at all. Maybe you're efficient and organized—more like Fran.

SOME OF US HAVE IT, SOME OF US DON'T

Fran runs her own investment firm and wrote the book, *How to Be Financially Secure in just 2,769 Easy Lessons*.

It's okay, you can relax. I'm not going to recommend that you read it. She never translated the book from Wall Street jargon to layperson's terms. Janet is easily intimidated by "tens" like Fran. As long as they stick to topics like kids, the latest news, weather, people, and places, she's comfortable, but where finances are concerned, they don't speak the same language. At times I wonder if they're even on the same planet.

Fran can't help it if she loves to work with figures. Budgeting is second nature to her. At fourteen, when most girls were spending their last dimes on anti-acne gels and designer jeans, Fran bopped into money markets and real estate. She's the kind of person who has never suffered nightmares over an unbalanced checkbook. Frankly, imbalances were simply never on her list of things to do.

Actually, Janet's checkbook balances, too—after she adds or subtracts the difference between her figures and the bank's. Janet would like to move up a few steps on the Financial Genius Scale, but—let's face it—turning a toss-it-in-a-drawer-til-tax-time type like Janet into a financial genius like Fran is . . . is . . . well, let me put it this way. Would you ask a leopard to lay eggs?

To Janet, a *bull market* is something that happens between the farm and the meat counter. And budgets? Janet tries, but it's probably best not to bring that subject up to her for another year or so. Remember the conversation she and I had at the beginning of this chapter? Well, a few days later during a phone conversation I commented that I thought maybe she should try a budget.

"Budget? Ha!" Her laugh bordered on hysteria. "The baby has been crying for the last three hours with colic. While I rocked her, Kevin (the two year old) poured a bottle of Joy in the dishwasher and turned it on. I'm having enough trouble keeping my mind in balance, let alone a budget. Oh no . . . not again! Kevin! Stop that!" The phone clattered to what was probably the floor.

A few seconds later Janet was back on the line. "Sorry about that," she said. "Listen, I gotta go. Kevin just plugged the hair dryer into our beagle's nose."

FINANCIAL WEIGH-IN

By now you may be viewing Janet's case, and maybe yours, as hopeless, but there really is hope. Besides, if you'll recall from the first chapter, we're in the process of examining the dark and dusty dead ends of our money maze and laying our financial burdens out in the open where we can assess the mess. After meeting Janet and Fran, where do you see yourself? Are you a ten like Fran, or would you see yourself more in the middle? Or, like Janet, do you see yourself tottering dangerously close to the edge of financial ruin?

Let's take a few minutes now to do a personal assessment. Below is a quiz to help you rate your money management skills and determine where you fit in the financial picture. Answer as you really are—not as you wish you were.

FINANCIAL AWARENESS QUIZ

	Yes	No	Sometimes
1. Do you worry about where you're going to get the money to pay your monthly bills?	[ ] 0	[ ] 2	[ ] 1
2. Do you often argue with family members over money?	[ ] 0	[ ] 2	[ ] 1
3. If you lost your present income, would you find yourself immediately in serious financial difficulty?	[ ] 0	[ ] 2	[ ] 1
4. Do you know exactly how much you owe?	[ ] 2	[ ] 0	[ ] 1
5. Do you ever spend money out of boredom, worry, or anxiety?	[ ] 0	[ ] 2	[ ] 1
6. Do you ever feel guilty over purchases you make?	[ ] 0	[ ] 2	[ ] 1
7. Do you often borrow money to cover emergency expenses?	[ ] 0	[ ] 2	[ ] 1
8. Are your credit card bills too high to pay off completely each month?	[ ] 0	[ ] 2	[ ] 1
9. Do you have an organized record-keeping system?	[ ] 2	[ ] 0	[ ] 1

10. Do you now operate within a budget?   [ ] 2   [ ] 0   [ ] 1

11. Do you know your current net worth?   [ ] 2   [ ] 0   [ ] 1

12. Do you keep a reserve savings account equal to four months or more of your current salary?   [ ] 2   [ ] 0   [ ] 1

13. Do you ever go shopping to feel good?   [ ] 0   [ ] 2   [ ] 1

14. Do you have investments set aside for retirement income (other than social security)?   [ ] 2   [ ] 0   [ ] 1

15. Do you always reserve enough money for tithing?   [ ] 2   [ ] 0   [ ] 1

Now go back over your answers and add up the numbers you checked. This will be your raw score. To find your rating on the scale, divide 3 into your raw score (i.e., 15 divided by 3 = 5). How did you do? I came out with a raw score of 21, which puts me at 7 on the scale. Take a moment and mark your outcome on the scale drawn below.

FINANCIAL GENIUS SCALE

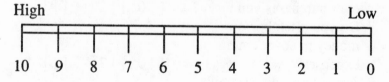

High   Low

10   9   8   7   6   5   4   3   2   1   0

A COMMON GROUND

Most people occupy a space in the middle of the scale (between seven and three) and could probably use help.

Scoring high on the Financial Genius Scale doesn't

mean, however, that we know it all, or that we are free of money problems. While a "ten" may do a commendable job of managing and investing money, he or she may be bottoming out when it comes to those heavenly treasures we've heard so much about.

In truth, we can be wealthy and debt-free and still find our relationship to money in direct conflict with our relationship to God. And that can be extremely hazardous to our spiritual health.

Janet and Fran are at opposite ends of the scale. They seem to have nothing in common. They handle money in different ways, but there is a common ground. They both desire it, need it, and like the things it can buy. They are both enslaved by it, and money, true to its reputation, has managed to encumber them and keep them from being fully committed to God. Both, too, have agreed that something must be done and have agreed to do whatever is necessary to set matters right.

TAKING THE FIRST STEP

Saving money and overcoming the obstacles in your money maze takes time, talent, and commitment. Most people are stuck in the money maze, because their problems are too big to handle. They don't recognize their abilities and potential, and they often lack commitment to follow through with goals.

Our friend Janet suffered from all of the above. She'd fallen into a depressive cycle and saw problems as overwhelming and out of control.

The key to winning the battle and successfully navigating the money maze is to fight one small battle at a time. Below is an illustration of the depressive cycle, as well as the optimistic cycle, into which our feelings, thoughts, and behavior can lead us.

DEPRESSIVE CYCLE

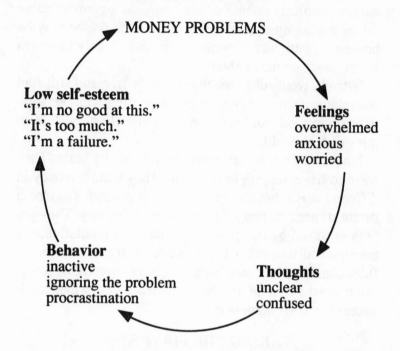

MONEY PROBLEMS

Low self-esteem
"I'm no good at this."
"It's too much."
"I'm a failure."

Feelings
overwhelmed
anxious
worried

Behavior
inactive
ignoring the problem
procrastination

Thoughts
unclear
confused

In the above diagram, we see that the focus, "Money Problems" is vague, broad, and difficult to grasp. At first, Janet was sure she could solve the whole of her money problems immediately. Then, with one failure after another, she became increasingly anxious and confused. Seeing herself as incapable of solving her money problems, she tried to ignore them.

"I'm a failure," Janet announced one day. "I know we should get our finances in order, but it's hopeless."

I showed the depressive cycle to Janet.

"That's it," she replied. "That's exactly what happens. But what can I do about it?"

I explained that to solve her money problems, she needed to move from the depressive mode into the optimistic cycle. "You can do that," I said, "if you follow these six guidelines."

1. *Break the overwhelming problem into small, manageable pieces.*

2. *Determine to accomplish one piece of work at a time.*

3. *Set reasonable, achievable goals for yourself in resolving each step.*

4. *Set specific measurable objectives.* Each objective should include the task you want to accomplish and the date you plan to do it.

5. *Set a deadline.*

6. *Be accountable to someone; i.e. a support group, a spouse, or a friend.*

"What's one facet of your money problem that bothers you?" I asked Janet.

"Well, maybe the way money disappears. It's so frustrating to come to the end of the month and not be able to account for hundreds of dollars."

"What could you do to keep track of the money you spend on a daily basis?" I asked.

"Keep an expense record, I suppose."

"Could you do that?" I asked. "Maybe for a week?"

"I'm not good at keeping records, but I guess I could do it for a week."

Janet won round one. With one successful venture on her record, she was on her way toward feeling confident about herself and her accomplishments. Now let's see what can happen when we deal with our money problem using the small step approach.

As you can see, Janet's more defined goal is to find out where the money goes for miscellaneous expenditures. Her objective (a first step toward reaching her goal) is to keep an expense record for one week.

OPTIMISTIC CYCLE

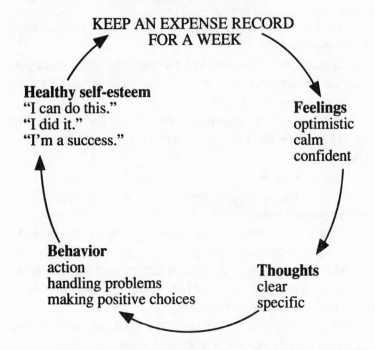

KEEP AN EXPENSE RECORD
FOR A WEEK

Healthy self-esteem
"I can do this."
"I did it."
"I'm a success."

Feelings
optimistic
calm
confident

Behavior
action
handling problems
making positive choices

Thoughts
clear
specific

By working through one portion of our money maze at a time, setting small attainable goals and specific objectives, we can maintain a higher level of control over our financial affairs. And that is exactly what we will do throughout this book. As you set out to take your first step, consider the following:

TIME TO CONSIDER

1. Discuss the outcome of your Financial Awareness Quiz with a friend or your support group.

2. Write your findings in your journal or diary. Seriously consider the areas in which you need help and list them.

3. Discuss the depressive and optimistic cycles. In which pattern do you most often find yourself? If you are caught in the depressive cycle, are you willing to change?

4. What are your most serious financial problems? You may have difficulty with overspending, lack of self-discipline, expensive habits, a love for clothes. Write these in your journal. They will serve as an indicator of your growth toward financial freedom.

5. Pray for one another, encourage one another, be honest, open, and real with each other as you seek your way through the money maze into financial freedom.

These first two chapters are perhaps the most important in the entire book, for unless we can commit ourselves to changing the way we think and feel about money, our efforts will be futile.

It's time now to enter another phase of the book. In part 2 we'll confront the obstacles (one at a time) in our money maze that block our path and cause us to lose our way amidst bad spending habits and rising debts.

Part II

Confronting the Monsters in Your Maze

At almost every turn in the money maze we run into creatures that gobble up our money before we can say "budget." Just for fun, close your eyes and imagine what your money-eaters look like. Are they like dozens of elusive mice scurrying in and out of your wallet, eating money as if it were cheese? Or, is your money-eater more like a fire-breathing dragon, who looms in your path and demands that you feed it everything you've earned and more?

If you're like most consumers, you may have versions of both. In the next two chapters we'll face these intimidating and frustrating enemies. We'll put them in their respective cages and limit their money intake.

3
...

Foiling the Money-Eaters

Is your money more elusive than the kids on cleaning day? Does your budget have more holes in it than a wedge of Swiss cheese? If so, the miscellaneous money-nibblers are probably holding you captive. For many people, the most debilitating factor in navigating the money maze is the way money disappears.

To move beyond the mice in our money maze, we'll need to assess the damage, arm ourselves with willpower, and put the little monsters on a strict diet.

When I first set up a budget and had to account for all of my expenses, the "miscellaneous expenses" column had more figures than a health spa. At first I blamed the money disappearance on my husband. "You're buying too many cups of coffee and newspapers," I accused. "And what about those daily Cokes and donuts?"

After a quick calculation Ron said, "My morning coffee and muffins comes to about sixty dollars, newspapers about twenty dollars. Add an occasional movie and lunch out brings me up to about one hundred dollars a month."

Ron's miscellaneous expenses accounted for about twenty percent, so I decided I'd better look at my own spending habits. I mentally inventoried the previous month's expenses, trying to remember where all the cash had gone.

Day one: loans, $5.00 (my daughter needed a little extra cash); two Diet Cokes, $1.50 (I have this addiction . . .); a Baby Ruth, 45 cents (I needed a sugar fix); bus fare, 50 cents; and a bagel with cream cheese for lunch on the run, $1.95. Hmmm, that was over $9.00 in one day, with nothing to show for it except a few extra pounds.

Day two: Diet Coke, 75 cents (I've got to quit drinking this stuff . . . but isn't everyone entitled to one vice?); Ultra Slim Fast, $8.99 (I decided to go on a diet); gas, $15.00; embroidery thread for my cross-stitch project, $3.40; picture frames for my grandchild's new photos, $15.00 . . . and . . . I couldn't go on. My memory went blank. Buyer's amnesia, I think they call it.

All I could recall was a blur of mini-marts, milk and bread trips, craft shops, cosmetics, toothpaste, books, batteries, car expenses, an occasional lunch with friends, and a long string of fast-food chains.

FAST-FOOD FACTS

As I thought about all the lost money, I realized that eating out had nibbled away a large portion of it.

In an interview with JoAnne Coughran, author of *Victory At the Supermarket*, she revealed some startling facts about fast foods. "Who's the biggest money-monger in the United States?" she asked.

I shrugged my shoulders and ventured a guess. "Del Monte foods?"

"The fast-food industry. And we're talking megabucks here. Did you know that McDonald's is the largest food producer in the world?"

"You're kidding!" I exclaimed. "Bigger than General Foods?"

She nodded. "Shocking, isn't it? Yet it's easy to understand when you consider that over half of the families in the United States eat more than fifty percent of their meals out. The average family eats out six times a week."

"Really?"

"Yes, and it's that quick-fix philosophy that gets us into trouble. Why waste precious time cooking when you can grab a meal in two minutes? And most people feel they're getting a bargain."

"Well, aren't they?" I asked. "I mean, a hamburger only costs about two dollars, and french fries . . . what are they? Seventy-five cents?"

"Compared to restaurant dining, yes, they do seem reasonable. However, when you compare fast-food prices to raw materials from the grocer, there's a big difference. As an example, for the cost of an average burger, you can buy a pound of hamburger, and perhaps the trimmings to feed four people. You can buy two or three times as many raw potatoes as you get in one side order of fries."

"I see what you mean."

Then we discussed the second worst money-monger—prepared foods, like pancake, biscuit, and cake mixes, frozen dinners, pasta preparations, and U-bake pizzas.

Occasionally, prepared foods can save overworked and busy families time, but so-called convenience foods are not always fast, and they are seldom as nutritious or as tasty as homemade. For example, I can whip up a thick, savory spaghetti sauce that tastes like it simmered all day in the time it to cook the noodles. The same is true for pancakes and waffles, and so called *helpers* for meat, fish, and pasta products. Most of us can turn out a terrific goulash in no more time than it takes to prepare the "prepared" food.

Before you buy convenience foods, consider the cost and the time saved as well as the nutritional value. If you can do a better job for less money in equal time, why pad the pockets of the food-makers? Here are some final thoughts on conquering the prepared food battles.

• Unprocessed foods are usually your best buys.

• Coupons for processed foods don't always guarantee a bargain.

• Compare raw materials to ready-made products as you calculate your available time and resources.

• Eat at home as often as possible.

• Use the most basic ingredients available.

• Keep plenty of staples on hand so you can prepare those "quickie meals" in your own kitchen.

• Avoid frequent pit stops at your local convenience stores. Instead, make a list and shop weekly.

• Simplify. Try cookbooks like *Living More With Less* by Doris Longacre, or *Diet for a Small Planet* by Francis M. Lappe.

Let's look at yet another hurdle in taming the money-nibblers: convenience stores and quick trips to the mall.

THE MINI-MART TEMPTATION

Convenience stores and malls with an abundance of stores all under one roof are handy. We can pop into the mini-mart for a gallon of milk or a loaf of bread. Or zip over to the mall for some hand cream, a sweater, and a shower curtain.

Easy access to these stores is a blessing when you need an item or two. They can, however, gnaw away at your unsuspecting budget. Few people have the willpower to buy the *one* item they came for.

Maybe you've wondered why it's so hard to stick to your list. Stores, like commercials, are designed to tempt you. You can almost hear them chanting, "Feast your eyes and fill your tummy. Let us handle all your money."

You think I exaggerate? Go ahead. Try walking in and out of a quick-stop store without purchasing more than you went in for. You need milk? It's in the back. There, past the ice cream and soft drinks, on the other side of the potato chips.

You made it back? Good, now let's see you maneuver past the greeting cards, the M&M's, and deep-fried chicken. You made it to the checkout stand? Wonderful, now you can read the seductive magazine headlines: "Roseanne's Amazing Five-Minute Diet," or "Learn the Uncensored Truth About Prince Charles' Unmatched Socks."

Okay, suppose you tear yourself away from the gossip racks. You still have to make it past the creamy caramels, Rice Krispies bars, and . . . and . . . oh no! A chocolate-glazed, custard-filled donut.

I didn't make it, did you? Following are four ways to resist the convenience store temptation. Don't go; blindfold yourself, plug your nose, and rent a seeing eye dog; borrow blinders from an understanding horse; take only enough money to buy what you need.

THE MICE ARE US

We can joke about how mice nibble away at our pocket money, but eventually we must face the somber reality that unless we gain control of our spending, we'll remain trapped in the money maze forever. Scripture tells us that if we are faithful in little, we can be trusted to be faithful in much. If we fail to manage the money God has entrusted to us, how can he trust us with true riches?[1]

As we scrutinize the nibblers scattered throughout our money maze, we see that the enemy is not as easily captured and discarded as mice. If we are honest, we see that the mice are formed out of our own attitudes, lack of organization and willpower, carelessness, laziness, and maybe even greed. The mice in our maze are us; we're the ones who must find a way to conquer our spending habits.

So how do we go about reducing the nibblers of our own making? We put them on a diet.

A TEN-POINT REDUCING PLAN

Before we can change the nibbling habits and curb our appetites, we need to find out what they are. Thus, the first plan of attack is to keep track of our expenses.

1. *Keep a record.* For one week, keep a notepad in your wallet or handbag. Write down and account for every penny you spend. Sound like work? It is. The purpose is not to create more paperwork for you but to help you see where your money goes. This process makes us aware of how much we spend and what we spend it on.

2. *Develop awareness.* As you record expenses, your awareness level sharpens. Once I became aware of certain habits, and because of my aversion to detailed record keeping, I spent less. For example, if I stopped for a soft drink and then remembered I'd have to record the expenditure, I'd mutter, "Forget it," and drive on. I became more and more alert to my habitual and sporadic shopping patterns. I also realized how much gas money came out of my cash supply. And speaking of gas, do you know how much it really costs to run an automobile? Cars don't just nibble money, they devour it.

3. *Keep it going*. One week of faithful record keeping will help you determine where your money disappears to, but you may want to take precautions so you won't fall back into your old patterns. It takes about a month to develop a habit and at least that long to break an old one. Make a pact to continue the records for one more week, then one more, and one more. There you have it—a month. By that time, recording your expenses will be routine.

At each week's end, record those miscellaneous expenses under the appropriate headings in your expense file or ledger. Anytime you eat out, even when it's at the "Golden Arches," list the expense under *food*. If you pick up a belt at a local boutique, the amount you spend should come under clothing. By the time you've finished, that nibbler called miscellaneous expenses will be slimmer than a gnat's elbow.

4. *Eliminate one at a time*. Each week of your diet program, eliminate one more money-eating habit. For instance, if you are a chronic mini-mart shopper, pass them by for a whole week. Then do a quick assessment. How did it feel? Did you miss them? Did you save any money by not buying items you didn't need? Remember, these quick stop shops and twenty-four-hour shopping weren't always available, and our parents and grandparents survived without them.

5. *Wait until tomorrow*. "Never put off until tomorrow what you can do today." Good advice—sometimes. For spending money, however, let's reverse it. To curb our instant gratification appetites, delete expenses, and reduce money output, we may want to change the saying to: "Put off buying until tomorrow what you can buy today."

A car dealer in our area finishes his commercials by saying, "If you don't come see me today, I can't save you any money." He's got it all wrong. If people *don't* go see him today, they'll save all kinds of money.

6. *Fritter money.* Once your miscellaneous expenses have slimmed down to a manageable size, you can ease off on your intense record keeping. Give yourself a weekly allowance for your odds and ends fund and don't worry about keeping track of every penny. It's okay to give yourself a small amount of cash to fritter.

When I'm on a food diet, I usually set aside a few calories for fun. I can use my saved calories for anything I want—like chocolate mousse or cheesecake. If I don't get an occasional treat, I get disgruntled and discouraged. Just so, the reward of fun money boosts my morale.

7. *Take only what you need.* Carry only enough cash to get you through the day. If I eat before I go to work and take my lunch from home, my money needs are zero. When goody-filled vending machines surround me, an empty pocketbook can save both my body's and my budget's diet.

8. *Reward yourself.* Suppose you manage to save ten dollars during week one, or even one dollar, or ten cents. Put that savings into a special account and watch it grow. Within a year you may have enough money to pay for a weekend retreat at the beach or a trip to Florida, Hawaii, or Europe. Or, it may just cover an emergency dental bill. You're right, paying for a dental bill is hardly a reward . . . unless you consider how relieved you'll feel when you can pay cash instead of adding it to your pile of bills.

9. *Spend it better.* The other day I stood behind a couple in the store who asked the clerk for seventy-five dollars in lottery tickets. I bit my lip. "You fools!" I wanted to scream. "How could you throw money away like that? There are millions of people starving in the world. Seventy-five dollars could feed a family of four for a week or two."

Then as I scooted into my car, I glanced at my purchases:

a Diet Coke and an almond fudge bar. I swallowed hard. I could have bought a half-gallon of milk or a pound of hamburger. I stood convicted. If I were to judge my neighbor for spending money on a chance, I'd have to judge myself for buying junk. Although the amount I blew was less, the sin remained the same. Maybe my fritter fund should go to feed the hungry.

10. *Discipline yourself daily.* Scripture says, "No discipline seems pleasant at the time, but painful. Later on, however, it produces a harvest of righteousness and peace for those who have been trained by it."[3]

We may not achieve a complete transformation overnight, but we can change "little by little, one step at a time."

TIME TO CONSIDER

1. Discuss the nibblers in your money maze with your support group or spouse. If you're traversing the money maze alone, list your specific spending problems in your diary.

2. Commit to using the Ten-Point Reducing Plan for one week. Report your progress to your partner(s) or chart in your diary at the end of the week.

3. What does it mean to discipline ourselves? Do a word study using the dictionary, a Bible dictionary, and a concordance. How often is the word used in the Bible? What implications does discipline have for us today? What steps can we take to become more self-disciplined?

4. Prepare a lifeline in case of failure. Read Matthew 14:22-33. Why did Peter fail? What did Jesus do? What message does this passage give to those of us who fail?

Lost in the Money Maze?

The account tells of Peter stepping out of the boat to walk on water. He takes a few steps, then sinks. Peter began his adventure by focusing on Jesus. His failure came when he shifted that focus to his fears and inadequacies.

When we fail, we need help to stay afloat. Christ provides that help. His strength will lift us up and keep us from sinking in our ocean of indebtedness. Our job is not to beat ourselves up, but to keep our eyes on Christ and on his strength and ability to transform us.

Reducing and sidestepping the nibblers in the money maze is rarely an easy task. It takes determination and time. As we make our way past the mice in our maze and enter the next chapter, we confront yet another money-eater—a dragon called "Charge."

4

...

Charging Your Way Through the Money Maze

This chapter is devoted to the one word that has come to mean more to the American public than Mom or apple pie. CHARGE! We face more avenues through which we can "buy now and pay later" than there are freeways in Los Angeles.

After all, buying on credit can get us what we want now without the age-old hassle of being able to afford it. Advertisers tell us we can stroll down easy street as long as we carry "the card."

I know, you're saying to yourself, she's going to tell me to cut up all my credit cards and live on a cash-only basis. Not necessarily. But it might help to look at what buying on credit entails so that we can make more responsible and godly decisions in our money matters. To do that we need to view credit buying with spiritual eyes that can penetrate credit's external virtues and bring to light the corruption that lies beneath the surface.

THE ENTICING WORLD OF CREDIT

Picture yourself wandering through your money maze. You've just shaken off half-a-dozen mousey money-nibblers and are rounding a corner you hope will lead to a passage marked exit. Instead, you come upon a lavish display of all the things you've ever wanted.

Take a moment and make a list of the items in that display. When you've completed your list, close your eyes and visualize the exhibit again. This time listen. Can you hear the voices beckoning you? One says, "Just try this leather-bound edition of *How to Produce Tsetse Flies for Fun and Profit* for fifteen days . . . it won't cost a cent."

Another says, "Imagine, a house full of furniture for only $7999.99, and you pay no interest for two full years."

What voices do you hear calling you to indulge in credit buying? Chances are, if you read magazines, newspapers, watch television, and/or listen to the radio, you could add hundreds more voices to the list.

CREDIT HAS ANOTHER SIDE

Buying on credit may be appealing, but it is also dangerous. What if every time you heard the word *charge*, you were confronted by a beast with watery red eyes, fiery breath, and a mouth the size of Mt. Everest? You'd run in the opposite direction, or at least approach with caution. Unfortunately, the dragons in our money maze, don't look like ole' red eyes—at least, not on the surface.

Rather, they appear as sleek, curvaceous red sports cars or Tom Cruise look-a-likes. Salespeople ply us with the stuff of dreams—a home of our own, a car that "hugs the road," a sailboat, a vacation in paradise, younger-looking skin, tan bodies that look great in loincloth, and, of course, fresh breath. The faces we see are beautiful and sensual and millions of people hear the call and follow. Advertisers convince us we should have it all—now! Even if we don't need it, can't use it, or can't afford it, we deserve it.

Sadly, the commercials show you fairy-tale beginnings, but never tell the rest of the story—which, in far too many cases, ends in disaster.

It's time now to tune out those enticing voices and look beyond the glamour. As we approach the display, we notice that it's only a set on a stage. Curious, we peek around the set and discover a cave with a gaping, ominous entrance. In the dimness a form appears. It's the dragon. Charge's red eyes glare at us. He spits fire out of his cavernous mouth in a final thrust to consume us.

Even without picturing the dragon in our maze, we know the commercials are an illusion. Yet we continue to allow ourselves to be seduced into believing that we can spend our way into happiness. Financial experts say that people who use credit cards buy about thirty-four percent more than they would without them.[1] Why? Perhaps because using a card doesn't have the same impact as spending cash. Or perhaps, as Ron Blue says in *The Debt Squeeze*, " . . . we choose to deceive ourselves and believe it could be true. The underlying motivation is the desire to meet a need for either security or significance."[2]

To move past the dragon in our maze, we need to take an objective look at Charge from all sides. In our examination we'll hear from three couples with three different experiences in handling their dragons. The first couple, Jenny and Adam, didn't see the dangerous side of Charge until it was too late.

A FAIRY TALE GONE BAD

Jenny and Adam, a young couple in their mid-twenties, discovered that beyond the bright lights and glamour of the buy-now-and-pay-later plan lay the hard cold facts of indebtedness. The congenial salespeople all too swiftly turned into scowling bill collectors. "We were so excited when we applied for credit and got it," Adam said. "We decided to buy a house."

"We didn't realize how much it takes to get started." Jenny sighed. "We needed living room and bedroom sets, a washer and dryer, a television set and VCR. But we did get nearly everything on sale. . . ."

"We were doing okay until Jenny's car died," Adam continued. "Then we had to get a new car—we couldn't get a loan on a used car and didn't have cash so we had to buy a new one . . . well, you know the rest."

Unfortunately, Adam and Jenny hadn't counted the cost. They borrowed money for the down payment on their $100,000 house and were making payments of twelve hundred dollars a month. In addition, they charged more than twenty thousand dollars on charge cards and personal loans. Their interest charges and fees on their credit purchases (not counting their home mortgage) came to around four hundred dollars a month. Adam lost his job and his insurance. Jenny got pregnant. They learned the hard way that while creditors love to lend you money, they hate it when you can't pay them back.

Their *Better Homes and Gardens* image of an affluent family crumbled. Adam and Jenny, hopelessly lost in their money maze, filed for bankruptcy. They lost their cars, their home, and a very large portion of their self-esteem.

CHOOSING NOT TO CHARGE

Because of the temptation to buy on credit and the danger of falling prey to the buy-now-and-pay-later plan, many money experts advise us to buy on a cash-only basis. Susan and George agree. They've been married fifteen years and have never bought anything, except for their home, on credit.

"To us," George says, "using credit cards and install-ment loans is like swimming in a crocodile-infested swamp. Sooner or later they'll devour your assets. It's a dangerous game and you stand to lose a lot more than your shirt."

"There's a certain freedom in paying cash for every-thing," Susan added. "If we need something we save for it. While we're saving, we comparison shop and look for specials. When we hand over the cash, that's it. We don't suffer headaches for months worrying about having enough money to make the payments."

"Didn't you have to borrow to buy your home?" I asked.

"Yes," George replied, "but we had saved twenty percent of the cost of the house for the down payment. Since we'd never charged and never had a bad debt, and we didn't have any outstanding bills, the bank considered us a good credit risk and loaned us the rest with the house as collateral."

"I think buying with cash is much safer and cheaper," Susan said. "If people buy on credit they need to be extremely well-disciplined to avoid overspending. They need to know what they're getting into and be aware of all the hidden costs."

POSITIVE CREDIT

George and Susan made some valid points. But not every-one agrees. Some financial experts feel credit, when used discriminately, is beneficial for our financial growth and development. They are referring to what I call positive credit.

Positive credit can help our financial situation and build our securities. Positive credit may include loans for a home or other real estate or a business venture. Borrowing money for investments like these, if done with wisdom, understanding, and prayer, may in time increase your net worth because your purchases will most likely increase in value.

Samantha and Bill use credit cards but use them wisely. "We know that buying on credit has its dangerous side," Bill says. "We use cards but pay off the balance every month."

"We have a good credit rating," Samantha added, "and if we need money for an emergency we can get it."

As Samantha and Bill say, some people use credit buying to their advantage. We'll talk about that shortly, but first let's look at negative credit.

NEGATIVE CREDIT

Negative credit stands for all those credit cards and installment loans that decrease in value. Cars, appliances, stereos, clothing, and so on lose value—practically overnight. Overuse of negative credit is hazardous, if not devastating, to your financial security.

In our society, however, buying on credit has become the norm. George and Susan say they didn't need a credit rating to get into their home. Some experts, too, agree. In fact, one authority says, "There is no such thing as a credit rating."[3] Others say establishing credit is a must. Who's right?

DO YOU REALLY NEED A CREDIT RATING?

One of the questions that arises when we examine buying on credit is the infamous credit rating. But before we discuss the credit rating, it might be wise to define it. A credit rating is a record of your past spending habits and paying performance. This information is collected by credit bureaus. Creditors use this rating to check on whether or not you can meet your obligations. A good credit rating simply says creditors can trust you to fulfill your financial obligations.

I agree with those who say you don't *have* to establish a credit rating. In fact, it's far too easy to establish credit. Often, all that's needed to get a credit card is a name, address, and phone number.

But I have spoken to several financial advisors who insist that a good credit rating is a must. One of these experts shared a story with me about a woman whose husband had died. She discovered that their credit rating had died with him. Without credit established in her name, she couldn't even lease an apartment or get a phone hook-up. I guess not everyone knows you don't need a credit rating.

Consequently, I've listed some ways to establish a good credit rating without falling prey to the dragon in your money maze.

HOW TO GET A CREDIT RATING WITHOUT FEEDING THE DRAGON

1. *Check your current credit rating.* You can easily do this through your bank, credit union, or a credit rating agency. If you find you don't exist as a credit-worthy consumer, and you'd like to, read on.

2. *Apply for credit at a department store in your name only.* Use your first and last name; i.e. Karen M. Warner, *not* Mrs. John Warner. This type of credit is easiest to get and the easiest to get into trouble with. If a credit card is likely to send you straight into the dragon's lair, you may want to move on to steps three and four.

3. *The next time you need to purchase a large item, such as a washer, dryer, television set, or microwave, buy it on a ninety-day, same-as-cash account.* Many retail stores offer this service to customers. You have three months to pay it off with no interest. If you save the money first and pay the monthly installments from your savings account, you'll establish credit without going into debt.

4. *Open your own low-cost checking and savings accounts, which offer a bank card such as MasterCard or Visa.* Some of the married women I've talked with own a separate account for household expenses. Talk with your husband about the pros and cons of such an arrangement. Once you have your own account, you can list the bank as a reference on loan applications.

A credit rating is only one consideration in determining whether or not you are a good credit risk. Creditors want to know if you have a stable income. You must also show that you have sufficient income to service your obligations. While credit may not be all bad, and while you may at times need a credit rating, we need to look at our ability to handle it.

BEFORE YOU SIGN THE DOTTED LINE

When you're playing with Charge, as with any dragon, you could get burned. Listed below are some basic anti-inflammatory precautions that may shield you in your encounters.

1. *Anytime you agree to use money through a loan, whether it's a credit card purchase or a direct loan, you'll receive a contract. Read it carefully.* Take it home if necessary. Know exactly what you will be paying, how it's figured, and when you'll be paying on it. If you can't understand it, ask. Be especially alert to finance charges, interest rates, and late charges.

2. *Lending institutions loan you money because they can make a fortune on fees and interest rates.* You are doing them a favor and are, in fact, helping to support them by letting them loan you money.

3. *Anytime you use a credit card you are borrowing money.* If you pay off the balance in full each month you pay no interest and, in some cases, may be using that institution's money for free.

4. *Interest rates vary, but most charge cards will run between fifteen and twenty-one percent on an average monthly balance or ending balance.* Put more simply, if you have a one thousand dollar balance revolving in a credit card account for a year, it costs you $150 to $210 in interest charges. I don't know about you, but I could find better use for my money.

5. *Borrowing money is not cheap.* While most businesses won't require your firstborn child, they will take all the money you're willing to give them.

6. *Buying on credit can expand your buying power when it is used within the guidelines of your budget.* It can ease the discomfort of expending large amounts of cash by allowing you to pay over a period of time.

7. *Before you borrow, be sure you can pay it back.* Your failure to pay probably won't result in your being thrown out to sea wearing concrete stockings—most creditors don't go that far—at least not physically. But from what people drowning in debt have told me, the mental anguish is worse.

HOW POWERFUL ARE THE DRAGONS IN YOUR MONEY MAZE?

In a world where plastic money is as good as cash and even a dog can be offered a credit card, it's easy to overextend ourselves. The line we walk between safety and disaster in credit use is as fine as the one we walk between holiness and sin.

What kind of line are you walking? Below is a quiz to help you determine how powerful the dragons in your maze really are.

		Yes	No
1.	Do you have six or more credit cards?	[ ]	[ ]
2.	Do you use three or more of those cards on a regular basis?	[ ]	[ ]
3.	Do you worry about whether or not you'll be able to make your credit card payments each month?	[ ]	[ ]
4.	Have you been operating in the red for two or more months in a row?	[ ]	[ ]
5.	Do you feel a pang of guilt when you pull out a card to pay for an item?	[ ]	[ ]
6.	Do you often charge, knowing you don't have funds in the bank to cover that amount?	[ ]	[ ]
7.	Do you buy small items on credit that you wouldn't or couldn't buy if you had to use cash?	[ ]	[ ]
8.	Do you often pay only the minimum required balance or less on your bills?	[ ]	[ ]
9.	Do you receive late notices?	[ ]	[ ]
10.	Does more than twenty percent of your income go for paying off credit or installment loans?	[ ]	[ ]
11.	Do you buy on credit when you are depressed to lift your spirits?	[ ]	[ ]
12.	Do your interest charges ever exceed the amount you're able to pay each month?	[ ]	[ ]

If you answered yes to one or two questions, you're

probably doing a fair job of staying out of the dragon's lair. Three to five yes answers indicates you've been flirting with danger and I'd caution you to step back now, while there's still time. If you answered yes to six or more, you're trapped in the dragon's den and will probably be eaten for lunch. If you find yourself in trouble with credit purchasing, here are some tips that can help you subdue your dragon's appetite.

HOW TO CONQUER
THE DRAGONS IN YOUR MAZE

Every dragon has its Achilles' heel, and those lurking in the depths of our money maze are no exception. Charge may have a commanding influence, but his resources are limited. He has only as much power as you choose to give him. You can limit Charge's monstrous appetite for your money by following these guidelines.

1. *Charge only in emergencies.* Use cash or checks whenever possible. And even if you'll *die* if you don't get that luscious silk jacket, you may need to say no. Wants and desires are not classified as a crisis.

2. *Reduce the number of credit cards you carry with you.* If you remain disciplined, and never charge more than you can pay off at the end of the month, you may want to keep your favorite cards. However, if you tend to overspend and have difficulty maintaining a budget, even one card can lead to disaster. For complete protection against the dragons, leave the cards at home, or better yet, destroy them and celebrate your freedom.

3. *Refrain from buying when depressed.* One woman, Angela, confessed. "Some of my weakest moments come when I'm premenstrual. During those down times I believe anything—that a thirty-dollar anti-wrinkle cream really works and that I deserve a complete make-over—

even if it costs a week's salary. While spending gives me a high, my spirits plummet when the reality of my spending spree hits me." You may also want to discover some less dangerous forms of enjoyment for your down days. Take in an art show, walk to the park, or read a good book.

4. *Shop but don't spend.* If shopping lifts your spirits, do it. Just don't spend any money. Impossible? Not at all. Leave your credit cards and checkbook and cash at home. Try on all the make-up, clothes, and accessories you want. Be extravagant; you're just looking. Whenever you find the perfect outfit, or whatever, for yourself or your kids, ask the clerk to hold it for you. Have your fling, then go home. If any of the items you encountered haunts you, go back in a day or two, when you're feeling stronger and take another look.

Try it. You'll be surprised at how quickly the love affair between you and your perfect hat ends. Usually, in these love-at-first sight encounters, absence makes the heart forget. My method gives shopping addicts a quick-fix, without the aftereffects of buyers remorse, anxiety attacks, and post-sale depression.

5. *Pay your entire bill each month.* The following two methods of doing this are almost pain-free. List each charge as you make it in your checkbook and subtract it from the balance. Beside each entry indicate which card was used. For example, MC = MasterCard; V = Visa; and so on. At the end of the month mark each entry with a yellow marker, total them, and add that amount back into your account. You then have enough money to cover your credit card bills. This method can help you cut down on credit card spending as well, if you follow one simple rule: *If the money isn't in the account, don't spend it.*

Another method that works well is to keep a small diary or notebook in your purse. In it list each of your charge cards by name. Set a limit for each and enter that figure under the name.

CREDIT CARD SPENDING RECORD

	Date	Visa	Date	MasterCard	Date	Nordstrom
Limit:		$100		$100		$40
	1/5	– 42	1/12	– 25	1/13	– 23
		$ 58		$ 75		$17
					1/27	– 6
						$11

As indicated, each time a charge is made, enter the amount and date under the appropriate heading and subtract it from the credit limit. When you've reached your limit, stop charging. Keeping track of your day-to-day charges makes you fully aware of where your money is going. These methods give you control of how much you want to budget, and you won't be devastated when your bills come due.

6. *Pay off your debts as soon as possible.* If you have allowed the dragon in your maze too much power, causing your bills to zoom out of control, here are several options:

• See about getting a consumer (or consolidation) loan. This will let you pay off your debts at a lower interest rate. If you must take this step to get out of debt, you must also discipline yourself to avoid debt in the future. Be willing to curb your credit spending significantly.

• Seek professional help. Most communities offer debt counseling through organizations such as Consumer Credit Counseling Service, a nonprofit organization, which can help you conquer debt problems, avoid bankruptcy, and handle money wisely.

IS BUYING ON CREDIT EVIL?

Some Christian pastors and financial experts believe buying on credit is going against godly principles. Others have said that buying on credit is a way of acting out their faith—trusting that God will come through with the money they need by the time the bills come due.

Used for the right purpose and with deliberate control, credit can make us good stewards of the money God allows us. Used wrongly, however, credit can easily become a corrupting power. Far too many are enticed by the illusions of having everything now without the worry of paying—until later. We want instant gratification. But the American dream of owning all too quickly digresses to a nightmare of owing far more than we are able to pay. We become slaves to a plastic god.

Next time you are tempted to buy on credit, ask yourself these questions:

1. *Is this really what God wants me to do?*

2. *How important is the purchase I'm about to make?*

3. *Have I confused my wants with my needs?*

4. *Am I really trusting God to provide, or am I acting like a spoiled child who spends extravagantly, expecting my daddy to rescue me?*

TIME TO CONSIDER

1. Consider the pros and cons of buying on credit from a biblical perspective. Proverbs 22:7 tells us, " . . . the borrower is a slave of the lender" (RSV). 1 John 2:15 says, "Do not love the world or the things in the world" (RSV). And Romans 13:8 reminds us that we should, "Owe no one anything, except to love one another" (RSV) .

2. Read and discuss the following situations dealing

with trust:

a. Kathryn and Joe had rented for five years. "We found the perfect house. We can't afford the thousand-dollar-a-month payment, but after praying about it, we decided God really wanted us to have the house. We decided to buy it and we'll just have to trust him to provide the money." Did God really tell them to buy a house they couldn't afford? Were they hearing God's voice? Their own desire? Satan?

b. Amy and Greg felt compelled to become missionaries. They were offered a position with a worldwide mission group to serve in Kenya. They didn't have the funds for the trip, but were told that if they felt this was God's will for them, that God would provide. Amy and Greg prayed earnestly and decided to quit their jobs and go, trusting that God would indeed meet their needs. Were they acting responsibly in trusting God?

Were the people in the stories wise in their handling of money? What might they have done differently?

3. Owing too much money produces stress, worry, anxiety, fear, and sometimes even dishonesty. Read Matthew 6:25 and Galatians 5: 1-26. How do the fruits of credit buying compare with fruits produced by walking in the Spirit?

4. Share with your group or write in your diary your own attitude toward credit buying. If you find that you lack discipline and self-control, or that you have acted like a spoiled and greedy child, make confessions to the Lord and to one another.

5. If God has reprimanded you about buying on credit, you may want to have a credit-card-cutting party. Celebrate your first victory over the dragon. Rejoice in the ability to advance to new beginnings in your money maze.

5
...

Bypassing the Bargain Bunnies

In the last two chapters we took some steps in overcoming the money-eaters in our maze. You've moved past the notorious nibbling mice and have learned to avoid the dragon named Charge. Your increased awareness of these dangers allows you to explore another passage in your maze. You see a light in the distance. Does it represent freedom? Or is it the light from another oncoming train?

You turn one corner and then another and there they are. The bargain bunnies! Why bunnies? Because I found the most cuddly stuffed bunnies for only twelve dollars each. I couldn't pass up the bargain and bought two. Besides, I needed another money-eater and bunnies fit the picture here. They are soft, cuddly, and innocent-looking. However, these irresistible, proliferating bargains greedily eat

67

us out of all the green stuff we're willing to part with.

Bargains come in the form of bunnies, clothing, furniture, and anything else we find a good deal on. Depending on how you use them, bargains can be a boon to our budget or an obstacle to financial freedom.

Few of us can resist a big sale. What if the couch you've drooled over for months is suddenly reduced to a whopping seventy-five percent off? The sweater you've watched all winter—fifty percent off. You can get two waffle irons for the price of one. You stop—naturally. Walking past a big sale like this is . . . well, if it isn't a sin, it should be. At least that was Janet's opinion when she went to the mall to buy her son a pair of jeans and came across "the sale to end all sales."

THE BIG SALE

Janet, still adrenalinized over her latest haul, dragged me into her bedroom to show me her purchases. "Isn't this precious?" she said, holding up a tiny ruffled dress. "Only ten dollars. I saved twenty dollars on it."

"That's great," I said. "Sarah will look adorable in it."

"Oh . . . well it doesn't fit Sarah. I . . . ah . . . thought it might, but . . . it doesn't matter," she added hastily. "My sister's having a baby in a couple of months. I'll need a gift for her anyway."

I guess my expression must have revealed my thoughts because Janet laughed nervously. "I know . . . what if it's a boy? Well, I'll save it for someone else. It never hurts to have a baby gift around for emergencies." Janet hurriedly hung the dress in Sarah's closet and drew another treasure from the mountain of bags covering the closet floor. "Wait till you see this."

Janet brought out shoes, slacks, jeans, sweaters, a collection of books (for when the kids get older), a bag of peach potpourri, and a dozen doilies (marked down from five dollars to two dollars each). After showing me her last purchase, a genuine cubit zirconium necklace, she collapsed on the bed. "You think I'm crazy, don't you? You're wondering what in the world I'm going to do with all this stuff. You're probably wondering why I'm hiding it in the closet, too. Well, I'll tell you why. Because Rob's going to kill me. I'll get the old, 'If you don't stop saving me money we'll go bankrupt,' speech." She paused for a moment and looked at me. "I really am crazy, aren't I?"

"Crazy isn't the word I'd use, Janet. A lot of people get caught up in the frenzy of buying. It's like they have to buy it now because they might not get another chance." I went on to reassure Janet and suggest she confess her binge-buying problem to the counselor she and Rob were seeing. She agreed.

ARE YOU "SAVING" YOURSELF INTO DEBT?

Most of us, at some time or another, have experienced the thrill of finding fantastic bargains, only to discover later that we "saved" ourselves into deep financial trouble. Certainly, purchasing items you need at a discount is commendable. In fact, in my first book on money management, I devoted several chapters to teaching my readers the fine art of bargain hunting. I realize however, that rather than learn how to find the best bargains, we might more easily negotiate the money maze by learning how to bypass the bargains—especially those we don't need.

Before we go on, take a look at your ability to resist bargains. Are you saving yourself into debt? If so, let's take some time to work on self-discipline and developing healthy shopping patterns. We've reached a difficult obstacle in our money maze. To successfully navigate through the enticing bargain basement, we'll have to protect ourselves with the armor of God's will, the sword of discipline, and the shield of simplicity.

WE HAVE TO SPEND MONEY

As we deal with finances, one fact emerges with amazing clarity. If we are to have the basic needs in life—food, shelter, and clothing, we have to spend money. As good money managers we want to get the most for our money—and that isn't always easy. As we approach a sale, any sale, we do well to pray that:

- God's will *will* be done.
- We'll resist temptation.
- Self-discipline will abound.
- We'll discern between our needs and wants.

We must spend money, but we can do it wisely. We can pause to ask God for his advice. And we can take it. Aside from equipping ourselves spiritually, we want to adapt some practical principles specifically designed for bypassing bargains that we don't need.

The Bible reminds us that "There is a time for everything."[1] For consumers there is a time for buying, and a time for saying no. To answer the question "How do we know what time it is?" let's look at Sally's method.

PLAN AHEAD AND PRAY

Sally needed, and had budgeted for, new drapes. A local department store quoted her $762.

An expert shopper, Sally comparison shopped and found a better price at a discount drapery outlet. They quoted $490, a $272 savings. But Sally had a budget of only three hundred dollars to spend on drapes. Before she began her shopping expedition, she had asked God to help her find some for that price or less.

"I'll wait for the Lord." Sally smiled. "He never fails

me." A week later Sally felt compelled to return to the discount store. She browsed through the ready-made draperies and found nothing. She then negotiated for better terms with the store manager and succeeded. "I can let you have them for $400," he stated. "Bottom line."

Sally sighed and said, "I'll wait." She made her way back through the sales table to check the specials one more time. There, on top of the pile, were her drapes—the perfect color, size, and style. "What a coincidence," the clerk told a beaming Sally. "I just put those out."

"That was no coincidence," Sally said as a feeling of satisfaction widened into a grin. Her heaven-sent price including tax came to $257. Sally saved $505 (a sixty-six percent savings) over the original quote. She proved beyond a reasonable doubt that it pays to shop around and, of course, to ask for a little help from a Friend.

I've had experiences such as Sally's myself. As I examined my wardrobe in preparation for winter, I realized I'd soon need a winter jacket. I shopped around from time to time but didn't find what I wanted in my price range. Finally, two months later, I found a $240 winter coat marked down to fifty dollars. I suspect the coat was actually worth about $140, but it was still a good bargain.

There is a broad element of trust and patience in buying within what I like to call God's timetable. Some years ago, when I first began writing, I needed a typewriter. I suffered from tendonitis and was severely limited by a manual typewriter. I needed an electric. With two hundred dollars cash and a prayer, I went looking. The only two hundred dollar typewriters I found were World War II vintage or older. I could have used my credit card and purchased a new one. Using the rationale that since God had called me to write, the money would be available to pay for it. That approach didn't feel right so I continued to pray and wait. I decided

71

that if God wanted me to have the typewriter he would supply my needs. Then one night, when I had just about given up, my husband said, "Let's call IBM." I laughed, but soon sobered when we discovered that the IBM dealer had gotten in a trade that day—a year-old Adler, top-of-the-line portable electric typewriter, pica type—exactly what I needed—for . . . you guessed it, two hundred dollars.

With prayer, patience, perseverance, and planning you can find what you need at a price you can afford. My husband and I rarely pay full price for anything. We find bargains on furniture, appliances, carpeting, clothing, food—everything. Here are some tips that tell you how.

1. *Make a list of the item(s) you need before you shop.* Check your budget and determine how much you can spend on each. Prioritize the list according to the greatest need. Pray. Present your needs before God and ask him to create a godly attitude in you about the shopping and those items you've listed.

2. *Check out thrift stores, secondhand shops, Goodwill, and Salvation Army stores.* You'll probably find them listed under "Thrift Shops," in your telephone directory. These are an excellent source for children's clothes, toys, and sometimes adult clothing too. On one visit to Goodwill, I found a Levi's shirt for my son for two dollars—new and never worn.

3. *Hunt garage sales for all kinds of treasures.* I have several friends who regularly hit garage sales and find great buys. If you're just beginning, I'd suggest making the first few trips with a seasoned garage-saler. I learned the business from my friend Lois. I've gotten books, puzzles, clothes, and gifts for pennies. The other day I found a turtleneck that looked like it had never been worn for seventy-five cents.

4. *Check your yellow pages for wholesalers and*

manufacturers. Look for key terms such as *factory outlet, samples, manufacturer, discount, bargain, used, and secondhand*. Before visiting manufacturers, call. They may not sell retail.

5. *Browse through the classified section of your newspaper for bankruptcy, garage, estate, clearance, factory close-out, liquidation sales, and auctions*. While these may point the way to real bargains, beware of companies that go out of business every week. Be aware, too, of what merchandise is worth before you shop. Some merchants have duped the public into believing they're getting something for nothing, when, in fact, they are getting nothing for something.

You can save by shopping for bargains. And sometimes you can add to your savings by negotiating for an even better deal.

6. *Haggle your way through the money maze*. " 'Utterly worthless!' says the buyer as he haggles over the price. But afterward he brags about his bargain!"[2]

I discovered the art of negotiating early in my marriage, when Ron and I went shopping for our first piece of furniture. Ron took the salesman aside and said "I'll give you forty dollars for it."

I couldn't believe he'd said that. The price tag clearly read sixty dollars. I backed away and pretended not to know him.

The salesman argued, "What do you mean forty dollars? It's already discounted at sixty."

"I know it," I mumbled as I slunk further from the action.

Ron ran his hand over the chair back and said, "Forty-five dollars cash. That's my final offer."

I closed my eyes, fully expecting the store manager to throw us out.

"Sold!"

"What!" I gasped and stared at the salesman. I inched my way back to Ron's side. "You mean it's ours? For forty-five dollars?" My embarrassment turned to joy as we carried our purchase out of the store.

Although I don't advocate telling anyone their product is "utterly worthless," I do feel that negotiating for a fair price is our prerogative as buyers.

7. *Practice age-old bartering*. Gardeners swap tomatoes for onions, farmers trade hay for ham. Even doctors barter. A plumber told his urologist, "You fix my plumbing and I'll fix yours."

Bartering gets people who need each other together. If you have merchandise, a skill, or a craft to share, you may want to barter. Some of my "moneyless" friends tell me, "Bartering gives us food, clothes, and a warm furnace. It can provide friends and jobs." Bartering can be fun and profitable, but beware, the IRS can tax bartered labor and goods. (Check your tax forms or your local IRS office for more details.)

8. *Do it yourself*. One way to bypass the bargain tables, especially if you have certain creative gifts, is to sew your clothes, service your car, paint your house, reupholster your furniture, and/or build your own bookcase or house.

We all have our specialties, and how-to books abound on everything from dog training to building your own hot tub. Before we embark on a project, however, we should ask ourselves these questions.

• Do I know what I'm doing?

• After figuring the cost of materials and time involvement, am I really saving money?

• Must this project really be done?

• Am I the best person for the job?

DEVELOP SALES RESISTANCE

Besides having patience and trust in God, and knowing when, where, and how to shop for bargains, you need to know when not to buy. This is called willpower, otherwise known as sales resistance. Blatant bargains have been known to affect people in bizarre ways. I've seen men and women, after waiting in line for hours, stampede through crowds and grab up sale items as though this were the last sale on earth.

Here are some ways we can develop sales resistance:

1. *When you see those drastic price reductions and feel your pulse race, STOP!* Close your eyes. Take a deep breath and say to yourself, I am in control. I will remain logical and level-headed. This is only a sale.

2. *Now open your eyes and check the item over carefully.* Some of the merchandise you encounter in discount stores are reduced because of inventory overload or a clearance of last year's models. However, much of it will be seconds—the not-quite-suitable-for-prime-time line. Note the workmanship on these items. Is there a sizing problem? Any flaws? Shipping damage? Sometimes the damage is minor, but the savings are great. We bought a Lane cedar chest for our daughter and saved one hundred-fifty dollars because of a small, barely noticeable nick on the back panel. Take care that you don't settle for poor workmanship and materials when you can find quality at comparable prices.

3. *Before you buy, ask yourself:* How much am I saving? Do I really need this? Can I afford it? If I say yes now, will I respect myself in the morning?

4. *Never buy an item you can't return unless you're certain it works or fits, regardless of how wonderful the price or how much you want it.* Always check with the

seller regarding refund policies. After all, what good is a half-priced chicken-plucker if it won't pluck chickens? Ask for a demonstration.

5. *Stop before you drop*. Exhaustion weakens your will-power. Shop when you are physically and mentally strong. Buy only what you need then leave.

I've used the phrase *buy what you need* several times in this chapter. Earlier on I also used the term *simplicity*. And as much as I'd like to leave this section of the money maze and travel onto safer things, I can't. We must deal with a certain aspect of shopping before we can move on; accountability in spending.

THE MALLING OF AMERICA

Why do we shop? Certainly there are times we need to, but what about those times when we shop for the fun of it? What compels us? What brings millions of people a day into the shopping malls across the country? A friend and I discussed the subject over coffee a couple of days ago. I told her about this book and my concern over the way shopping has developed as a way of life.

"America is being malled," I said. "What bothers me most is that I'm as vulnerable as the next person. I came to that realization the other day."

"What happened?" Nancy asked.

"Well, there I was, walking through Vancouver Mall, dodging a swarm of teenagers. Suddenly it hit me. I had no idea what I was doing there. I thought back and real-ized I'd been writing and got depressed. I couldn't work so I went to the refrigerator. Then I grabbed my coat and headed out the door."

"So . . . you needed a change of scenery."

"Yes, but the mall? I could have gone to the park or to the river. Anyway, since then I've done a lot of thinking. I really believe God is telling me to be more careful about how I spend my money—that I've been buying a lot of things I really don't need."

"I know what you mean. Lately, the things I used to feel were important seem so frivolous. I've really cut back."

"Me, too." I paused and took a long drink of tea. "Part of it, I think, is that the more I abandon myself to God, the less important material things are. I also think this has something to do with the worldview I'm developing."

DEVELOPING A WORLDVIEW

I went on to explain that I look at my situation in relation to people in other countries and cultures. When I compare myself to the average American, I'm somewhere in the middle class. But when I put myself next to an African whose average income is twelve dollars a month, I'm wealthy.

So I begin to look at my life and my accumulation of treasures and wonder how I can help balance the scale. What can I give? How can God best use what I have to his glory?

DEVELOPING A GODLY VIEW

When we view buying from God's viewpoint, we will almost always be faced with the questions: *What do I really need? And am I managing God's resources his way?* We will also discover the awesome truth that God holds us responsible for what he gives us. This is a difficult topic. I struggle daily with the accountability-factor myself. It's also a personal dilemma because needs vary from one person to another. God deals with us in different ways and at different times. While I can't judge you for what you buy and how you manage your money, I can encourage you to ask God to show you his will for your life.

Having talked about developing God's view and a

worldview, I would be remiss not to also tell you that abstinence from buying is not a simple matter. I don't know all the answers. For that matter I don't even know some of the questions.

Were you to come into my house, you'd see those two fat, floppy-eared bunnies I told you about earlier, sitting on my couch. They aren't necessities, but the grandchildren love them and they certainly are a delight to hug. On further investigation, you'd find a television and VCR, a stereo, a mop doll, three porcelain dolls, and a lot of other things I could place on a things-I-don't-really-need list. I can't say that I wouldn't ever buy something frivolous to add to the collection. I like to think that God doesn't mind that we have a few toys to play with—as long as we don't get too many or hold on to them too tightly.

Passing through the bargains in our maze is hard, especially when we can't get through the door because we're so loaded down with all our treasures.

TIME TO CONSIDER

1. Take a moment to consider how much time you spend shopping in a one-week period. Was it time well-spent? Do you wish you had used the time differently?

2. List the items you purchased (excluding staples) during that week. Beside each item write "N" for needs (basic living expenses) and "W" for wants. Is God urging you to trim down your list?

3. Read the parable of the talents in Matthew 25:14-30. What does the story tell us about money management? What were the rewards? The punishments? How do you feel about the way the Master handled each case? Consider how God might feel about the way you handle the

money he has given you.

4. Work on developing a worldview. Consider this quote:

Our refusal to merchandise in the frivolous is directly connected to the high value we place upon human life. It is a wrong use of the world's resources to fritter them away on trivialities when human beings need to be fed, clothed and educated. We value people more than ostentatious clothes and gaudy homes. So long as the gospel needs to be preached, so long as children need to be fed, Christians cannot afford to have any part with the 'Vanity Fairs' of this world.[3]

Pray for a godly view . . . for insight to help you distinguish needs and wants and to do what is right in God's eyes.

6
...

Earn Your Way over the Top

Were you able to let go of enough excess baggage to allow you to squeeze through the narrow door on the other side of the bargains? Have you managed to stay ahead of the dragon named Charge and the miscellaneous mice in your maze? If so, you're ready to forge ahead. As we journey through our money maze, we come to an ivy-covered brick wall. Another dead end.

As we examine the wall we find a crude door that is slightly ajar. We push against it, but it won't budge. Our financial burden is too big to allow us to squeeze through the narrow opening.

Where do you go from here? You've done your best to save money. Perhaps you even cut up your credit cards. But you still don't seem to have enough money to support your expenses. Unfortunately, cutting back on spending is only one of the problems we need to overcome in order to escape the money maze. There are two ways to move beyond the brick wall in our maze. We can increase our income and earn our way over the top, or we can adjust our living expenses enough to make it through the door. Or maybe we could find a way to do a little of both. Before we explore the possibilities, let's look in on Janet and Rob to see how they're coping with the brick wall in their maze.

Janet chewed the tip off the only long fingernail she had left. She glanced at Rob. Slouched in his chair, her husband stared, unseeing, at the poster on the wall beside the door. The picture showed a kitten clinging desperately to the branch of a tree with her two front paws. The caption beneath it read, "Hang in there, Baby!"

We're trying, Janet said to herself, wondering if she and Rob hadn't already fallen. The credit counselor's fingers raced across a calculator keyboard adding up their fate. The credit counseling service was their last hope. If they couldn't get their financial situation straightened out here, they'd have to declare bankruptcy.

The clicking stopped and Janet took a deep breath to prepare herself for the worst. "Well," she said, "what's the verdict?"

"We might be able to help you," the counselor said as she turned the work sheet around for them to see. "You have three thousand dollars coming in each month, but forty-five hundred dollars in expenses. We can probably cut that back, but you'll still need to come up with five hundred to one thousand extra dollars a month. Can you do that?"

Rob straightened and leaned forward. Janet groaned. They were both working full-time. Earning that much more a month seemed an impossible task.

The counselor handed them a card. "I'm sorry I couldn't

give you better news. Why don't you think about it for a couple of days and give me a call? There are a lot of ways you can pick up extra cash."

"How—rob a bank?" Rob muttered as he took the card and shrugged into his jacket.

What do we do when there just isn't enough money? This isn't a problem only for the poor. In fact, I know some people whose income is eight hundred dollars a month, and they say it's enough. On the other hand, I've seen millionaires cry because they can't make ends meet. Sometimes the answer to our lack of sufficient cash is, as the credit counselor suggested, to earn more.

EARNING EXTRA INCOME
WITHOUT ROBBING A BANK

There are as many ways to earn extra income at home as there are tadpoles in Burnt Bridge Creek. In this chapter we'll only skim the surface, but the samplings may stimulate you into starting a whole new career. While these money-making ideas probably won't make you rich and famous, they certainly can help put some extra change into your empty pockets.

No matter what age you are or what you do, if you're looking for money-makers, you're on the right page.

You'll notice I said any age. Are you still active at sixty-five and eager to earn your way? Be Grandma for a day—with pay. In other words, baby-sit or house-sit. Pet-sit?

Whatever your age, you're too young to retire. Offer services for hire. Do you like to sew? My friend Marie works in her home as a seamstress. Besides sewing clothes for half the town of Battle Ground, she mends clothes and does alterations. She also sews costumes for a costume shop. Marie even created an evening gown for one of the contestants in the Miss Washington pageant.

Lost in the Money Maze?

What do you do best? Tennis? Writing? Pottery? Weaving? Singing? Turn your hobby or area of expertise into a profitable business venture by offering classes in your home or selling your creations.

Do you have an aptitude for math, a foreign language, or English? Tutor a needy student. To spark your imagination, I've concocted a chart. On the left, locate your special gift or interest. The column on the right tells you how to turn talent into treasure.

What I do best	How to make money doing it
Talk on the telephone	Telephone sales; answering service.
Cook/serve	Catering service; package and sell specialty foods such a cookies, bread, and so on.
Work with numbers	Bookkeeping/accounting; offer to balance checkbooks.
Type	Typing service: manuscripts, themes, term papers.
Sing	Give lessons; sing at weddings, funerals, anniversaries; deliver singing telegrams dressed as a chicken.
Grow things (plants, not babies)	Hang a shingle: "Plant doctor"; winter over plants in your greenhouse; grow and sell herbs or anything else.
Calligraphy (or other art)	Sell it; teach it.
Photography	Photojournalism; set up a studio and offer passport pictures, portraits, wedding photos, or other special occasion pictures.

Interior decorating	Use your home as a model, then advertise your talents.
Needlework	Create and sell your embroidery; teach knitting, crocheting, needlepoint, tapestry, or quilting.
Write	Be a newspaper stringer; write a how-to book; free-lance copy-edit, proofread, or index.
Read	Be a book reviewer.
Sales	In addition to garage sales and so on, be a part-time sales representative; or, if you have a great idea people can't live without, sell it by mail. (Check U.S. postal regulations first.)

By using these suggestions and/or coming up with some of your own, you may be able to leap easily over the brick wall in your money maze.

GETTING OVER THE WALL TOGETHER

While earning money and getting out of debt are important, we want to be careful not to sacrifice relationships in the process. You may work day and night to earn enough money to meet your expenditures, only to find it cost you your family and friends.

Janet and Rob are a good example. Rob took on a second job. Janet worked full-time. They told themselves it would only be temporary. They managed to earn enough money to meet their expenses but rarely spent time together as a family. Even more rare were the times they spent as a couple.

"We both became angry and resentful," Janet mused. "I

was so unhappy. I liked my job but missed the kids and felt guilty for not being a better mom. I was so tired of trying to do it all."

"I felt all of that and more," Rob admitted. "I kept thinking I should be able to do better. I was convinced there was something wrong with me. Why couldn't I make enough to support my family? It shouldn't be like this. I felt trapped."

"Me, too. We were at each other all the time." Janet glanced at Rob. He reached over to take her hand.

"What happened?" I asked. "I mean, you look happy enough now."

Rob cleared his throat. "Well, I guess it all blew apart when I didn't come home one night."

"I got really worried and called the pastor. He sat with me until Rob came home. We had a lot of time to talk and I told him about all the problems we were having with finances and . . . well, he was so nice. I expected him to tell me how terrible we were for getting into debt. But he just sat there and listened. He assured me we could solve our money problems without destroying our family."

"When I got home," Rob said, "I felt pretty rotten. I'd just gone down to the river to think. I realized we couldn't go on. I decided to quit my night job and have Janet go back to part-time. When I got home and found Janet and the pastor talking about the same thing, we felt like God was okaying my decision."

"It looks like you made the right choice," I said.

"Yeah," Rob grinned. "The money problems are still there, but I think we're making progress. We let my truck and the fifth wheel go back to the bank and sold a lot of things we didn't need. We're working hard to break some of our spending habits. The credit counselor thinks we might be able to work things out so we don't have to file bankruptcy. I think God values our wanting to get this money situation under control—but I think he values our relationships more."

Janet and Rob are fortunate. Many young couples fall into the trap of thinking that they'll work long hours now so they can have a nice house and cars and will catch up on their family-time later. Sadly, later seldom comes until it's too late.

We've talked of methods to help you earn your way over the wall, but also faced the danger that too much time spent on money-making efforts can strain, or even destroy, relationships. As Janet and Rob came to understand, earning your way over the wall may not be the answer.

Let's look at an alternative. G. K. Chesterton once said, "There are two ways to get enough: one is to continue to accumulate more and more. The other is to desire less."

Can we reduce our expenses by desiring less? Can we cut back to a more basic and simplistic life-style so that our expenses more easily fit in with the income we have? Can we make it through the slender opening in the wall? Maybe. Let's look at some possible ways to reduce our expense burden.

"DARE TO DUMP IT!"

The first step in cutting back is to liquidate some of our assets. By getting rid of what you don't need, you can simplify your life and make money at the same time. Perhaps the most obvious way to do that is to have a garage, attic, yard, auction, or estate sale.

"But what can I sell? Where do I start?" If those are your questions, read on.

To begin, take inventory. The best time for a garage sale is after spring-cleaning. Go through every room, drawer, closet, and cupboard for items you no longer use. This is no time for nostalgia. Sure your fourteen-year-old's baby stroller brings back memories of the way he was, but he outgrew it twelve years ago. I used to think I would save all my kids' baby things for my grandchildren. When they got to their teens I'd look at all the infant paraphernalia and get blubbery. *My babies are growing up. Soon they'll have little ones of their own, and I can get rid of this stuff.* With that thought I'd go into shock and pray the babies wouldn't come too soon. I finally sold everything at my garage sale.

If and when my grandchildren need these baby items, who knows, maybe I'll find them at *your* garage sale.

As you sort through years of collected trash and treasures keep this theory in mind. In *Sidetracked Home Executives*, Pam Jones and Peggy Young suggest that if you haven't "cooked with it, danced with it, sat on it, squeezed into it, mailed it, read, or watered it in the last twelve months . . ." you probably never will, so pitch it.[1] Their motto is, "Dare to dump it." Make it yours, too.

As you explore your home for possible saleable items, keep in mind the more popular attractions to garage sale customers. Merchandise that sells well includes antiques, books, linens, kitchen items, children's toys and baby equipment, memorabilia, and bookcases.

OBJECTS D'ART AND OTHER FINE SALEABLES

While you may not make a bundle selling your throwaways, money can be made on antiques and other collectibles. Recently a couple discovered that a painting they'd had hanging on their wall for years was a valuable work of art. Not only had it been painted by Van Gogh, but it sold for more than a million dollars. The chance of finding a rare and valuable painting is about as big as winning the lottery, but it happens.

What about your own art? Suppose in your house inventory you come across ten years' worth of art or craft projects you've created. While these fine art objects don't usually bring top dollar at garage sales, you may be able to sell them at a profit in local art or craft shows or even your own home salesroom.

Arts and crafts, by the way, provide excellent part-time income. Think of the possibilities. You can stay at home (except for occasional art shows and sales), enjoy your favorite hobby, and make money all at the same time.

Reducing your inventory may not make you rich or even get you out of debt, but it can give you the incentive to clear your home of excess weight and alert you to the truth about earthly treasures. I'm amazed at how quickly an item I once thought I couldn't live without turns into a worthless piece of junk I can't wait to unload.

FINDING EXTRA MONEY AROUND THE HOUSE

In addition to simplifying our lives by reducing our hoard of treasures, we can check our living patterns for additional ways to save money. Below are a dozen ideas that might help.

Save on utilities

1. *Have your home's insulation checked and updated.* Poorly insulated homes can cost a fortune to heat. Storm doors and windows also reduce heat loss. Insulate your water heater to cut down on water heating costs.

2. *During the cold season, keep the thermostat set at sixty-eight to seventy degrees.* Turning it down to around sixty degrees at night and when no one is home can save you even more.

3. *During warm weather, keep your home cool by closing windows and blinds.* Use an air conditioner only to keep the room comfortable (around seventy-eight degrees), not cold.

4. *Use fluorescent lights rather than traditional bulbs.* They last longer and use less electricity.

Save on food

5. *Lighten up.* Most of us can save money by buying and eating less food. Unless you make good use of leftovers, buy and prepare only enough for one serving for each person. And since the majority of Americans are overweight, it probably wouldn't hurt us to cut back to two meals a day.

6. *Lower calories, cholesterol, and save money by eating less meat and more vegetables, legumes, fruits, and grains.*

7. *Eat in more often.* Use less prepared foods.

Save on clothing

8. *Cut dry cleaning bills.* When possible, use bulk dry cleaning or wash items such as woolens and silks by hand.

9. *Wash and rinse most laundry with cold water.*

Save on automobiles

10. *Purchase used cars rather than new.* Most new cars depreciate thousands of dollars in value the moment they're driven off the lot, and even more during the first year. (Be sure to have the used car checked by a trusted mechanic before you buy.)

Save on other items

11. *Buy books from used bookstores at half price or less—or use your local library.*

12. *If you have a large house, consider house-sharing or taking in a boarder.*

I'm sure we can find many other ways to cut back when we begin to think in terms of living a simpler life-style.

Whether we choose to earn more money to meet our expenses, to lessen our expenses to fit our income, or to do both, one thing is clear. We will want to escape to the other side of the wall.

How? I wish I had an easy answer. I don't. At this wall we face some of the toughest decisions we will ever make. Do we strive to earn more money, or do we strive to imitate the simple life of Christ? Can we do both? Do we sacrifice relationships with our family and God in order to maintain a certain preestablished life-style? Or do we choose to nurture relationships at the risk of losing our possessions?

We can find some of our answers by understanding more about the matter of simplicity. Simplicity has many meanings. It carries the idea of clarity, directness, innocence, and honesty.

The heart of simplicity is in living your life with Christ at the center. Too many obligations, worries, and stresses shift our focus from God to the world. We become strained, unhappy, and oppressed. We struggle for truth but can't see it because our complex life-style has pushed God aside. Without God in the center our view is distorted and confused.

It will take time to sort through the confusion we find at the wall. We certainly can't expect to resolve something so difficult in the few words we have left in this chapter. We can, however, look for ways to simplify our spending patterns and balance our income and expenses. We can learn to put our finances in order through customized budgeting and record keeping, and that's just what we'll be doing in the next few chapters.

TIME TO CONSIDER

1. If you, like Janet and Rob, need to bring in more cash, brainstorm with your spouse or support group ways

to earn extra income to see you through your present debt problems.

2. As you read Janet's and Rob's nearly tragic story, what were you thinking? What are your priorities regarding time and money? Are you sacrificing relationships in order to keep making enough money to pay your expenses?

3. Take some time to get in touch with your feelings about this chapter. How can you get beyond the wall? Which way do you think God wants you to go?

4. While you may not be able to change to a simpler life-style overnight, you can regain simplicity of the heart. Spend some time alone to meditate, read scripture, listen to sacred music, walk in the forest, or just sit still. Exclude every problem, pressure, or person from your thoughts. Concentrate on God alone. Pray. Be silent. Listen. Allow him to enter the core of your being. Feel yourself become one with God and know that this is simplicity of the heart. This is where we come for answers knowing that, when we ask, God will answer.

Part III

Putting Your Finances in Order

As we leap over the wall with extra earnings, or pass through the narrow passage by eliminating more of our assets and gaining simplicity of the heart, we find ourselves in another wing of our money maze. The way is dark and damp. We hear water lapping on a nearby shore. Brooding swirls of murky water pulse toward us. An ominous ocean of debt bars our way. Unpaid bills, credit cards, personal loans, tax mortgages, and discarded budgets threaten to flood us with discouragement.

Financial freedom lies in the distance. We want to cross but aren't sure how. We have several options. We could go back—forget about our commitment to free ourselves from the money mess. We could try to swim the expanse. Or, we might build a barge to carry us across.

Since we've come so far, I doubt you would really want

Lost in the Money Maze?

to give up. And with the weight of those financial burdens hanging around your neck, you won't want to swim, so that leaves the boat. If that's your choice, then grab your pad and pencil. Our first step in crossing the bill-littered water is to build a leak-proof budget.

7
...

Building a Budget

Budgets determine whether we sink or swim in the financial sea of life. Everyone who lays claim to financial freedom works within a budget. Even the government—well, let's just say they have one. Financial experts agree that the chief cause of financial failure is the lack of proper budgeting. Yet some people, when faced with the prospect of having to work with a budget, turn pale, nauseous, and break into a cold sweat.

As you've probably guessed, we're about to concentrate on building a budget. Before we do that, however, let's deal with a few underlying problems: certain misconceptions, rationalizations, and negative attitudes toward living within a budget.

WHO NEEDS A BUDGET?

Elizabeth, an artist and divorced mother of two, hates keeping a budget. "It's too restrictive. I don't like being controlled by a bunch of numbers."

Alice, another budget-hater says, "Keeping a budget is about as exciting as operating the stopwatch at a snail race."

"I can't stay with a budget so why try?" Kathryn confesses. "If I don't do it, I won't feel like a failure."

Few people really enjoy budgeting. In fact, that's one of the reasons I chose to wait until now to discuss it. Before presenting the paper problems I wanted you to first develop some preliminary skills and successes in saving and managing money.

Contrary to popular belief, budgets are not necessarily restrictive. Rather, problems surface when we view budgeting from the wrong perspective. A budget is a plan or goal—an estimate of our future income and outgo. It can be as simple or elaborate as you want to make it.

Budget styles vary from one individual to another. While some need minor guidelines, others require boundaries as heavily guarded as Fort Knox. Penny falls into the "minor" category. "I never write out a budget," she says. "I don't need to; I have it memorized. I know exactly how much I bring in and pay out each month. My budget has been the same for years."

For Prudent Penny, the mind-over-money philosophy works fine, mostly because she plans ahead and never overspends. If, however, you run out of money before you run out of month, you may need a more structured method. Without restrictions, you could spend yourself down the river and drown in the ocean of debts.

Not everyone (especially self-disciplined people like

Penny) need an extensive budget. But we all need a plan to help us live within our means.

DESIGNER JEANS AU GRATIN

A young couple recently discovered the importance of budgeting. Their teacher? Experience. Nancy and Jim had enjoyed four short months of honeymoon when Jim flew out of town on a business trip. During his two-week absence, Nancy received both of their paychecks and instructions from Jim to pay the bills. Since the banks had closed, Nancy cashed the checks at a local supermarket. "I'll deposit the money that's left tomorrow," she reasoned.

While Jim took care of business in Ohio, Nancy managed the money. She *managed* to sidestep the bank deposit, forget the bills, and spend the whole bundle. In addition, Nancy *managed* to run up more than forty-five hundred dollars on her Visa card.

By the time Jim returned, Nancy didn't even have enough money left to buy ingredients for dinner. She greeted her travel-weary husband at the door with, "Hi, Honey! How do you like Designer Jeans Au Gratin?"

As Nancy confessed her accidental spending-spree, Jim turned red.

"How could you do this?" he shouted. "It will take at least a year to pay off these debts. What did you buy?"

"Things," Nancy winced.

"Things! You spent six thousand dollars on *things*?"

"Well . . . I wanted to surprise you. I painted the bedroom and got new drapes and a chair. I found a great buy on a new sewing machine. And you know I've been wanting a digital radio alarm—Sears had one on sale. Now we can wake up to music instead of that horrid buzz. And best of all," she finished proudly, "Sak's had a fabulous sale. I bought you some shirts and pants and found my favorite designer jeans for only forty dollars a pair. I saved more than two hundred dollars."

"That's great!" Jim ran a shaky hand through his hair. "At least we can go bankrupt in style."

Nancy frowned and chewed her lower lip. "Jim, I'm sorry. It's just . . . well, I was lonely without you. I didn't mean to spend the money—it . . . it sort of disappeared. Jim . . . ." She approached him cautiously. "We could borrow some money from Dad."

"No!" he snapped. "We'll handle it ourselves."

"I'm sorry." She sniffed. "Can you ever forgive me?

Jim's voice softened. "Look, Honey, it'll work out. Besides, I have an idea—we'll take it all back—except for the paint."

"Huh? Oh, yeah! I hadn't thought of that. Uh oh. The jeans. I can't return them—final sale."

Jim pulled her gently into his arms and grinned. "That's okay, as long as I don't have to eat them."

"What?" Nancy frowned.

"The jeans. You asked me if I liked Designer Jeans Au Gratin. Actually, Jeans a la Nancy suits me better."

Nancy and Jim spent the rest of the evening forgiving and forgetting. They made plans for a new future with an adjusted budget, which, Jim advised, they would work on together.

Not every misappropriation-of-funds case can claim a happy ending. Some end up in divorce, bankruptcy, or even jail.

As I said earlier, a budget doesn't have to be time-consuming or elaborate. If you've never kept track of your spending before, however, the first few months could prove demanding. But once the budget is set up, the time you spend on it is up to you.

PRIORITY BUDGETING

Now that we've established the importance of a budget, let's get on with the business of building one.

The first consideration when planning a budget is priorities —what's most important in your family. As your needs vary, so will your respective budgets. The only common ground we all have in establishing a budget is a limited income. We must live within that income boundary.

Paradise Lost

This phrase became startling reality to my friend Jennifer. Last year she lost not only her financial security but her husband. A boating accident left her husband, Tom, in critical condition. After eight months of intensive care, he died.

Before the accident, Jennifer and Tom managed well on his sixty thousand dollars-a-year income. Their priorities included a modern country home complete with horses, two new cars, a sailboat, and two trips a year to "paradise." For Jennifer, paradise and a lot of other things were lost. Medical bills had eaten away most of the family's assets by the time Jennifer secured a job. Going from sixty thousand dollars a year to sixteen thousand was a tremendous struggle. But Jennifer shrugged her shoulders and said, "Guess we'll just have to tighten our belts and simplify."

Let's look at Jennifer's simplified budget (see fig. 1).

Lost in the Money Maze?

ITEM	INCOME	EXPENSES	TOTALS
Salary (after taxes)	$ 1,200		<u>$ 1,200</u>
Total income			<u>$ 1,200</u>
House payment—including taxes		$ 650	
Second mortgage		200	
House insurance		50	
Car insurance and license		50	
Loans:			
a. Roof repair ($200)		50	
b. Attorney fees ($4,500)		100	
c. Medical bills ($8,000)		100	
d. Car payment		200	
Child care		150	
Groceries (for four)		300	
Utilities		100	
Telephone		40	
Medical/dental		120	
Transportation (gas)		70	
Clothing		<u>50</u>	
Total expenses		$ 2,230	<u>$-2,230</u>
Total over/short			<u>$-1,030</u>

Figure 1

Even after Jennifer trimmed the frills from the family's previous budget, she had to cut even deeper to make ends meet.

"The hardest part about all this," Jennifer confesses, "is facing the bill collectors. I tell them I'll pay if it takes me the rest of my life. Most of them are satisfied with that. They'd rather be paid a little than not at all. But some of them," she groaned, "make me feel like a criminal."

"You sound determined." I felt a little envious. "I wonder if I could be so brave."

"At first it seemed overwhelming. Then I sat and wrote everything down—all our assets and liabilities. When it was all on paper, I started listing the things I could sell and narrowed the list down to what we really needed." She sighed. "Now it looks like I'm down to selling my family in order to pay those medical bills."

My questioning look brought a twinkle to her eyes as she explained. "My horses. Not the kids—although . . . nah." She shook her head and laughed.

Jennifer has listed her home for sale and hopes to make her income and budget more compatible within the year.

I used Jennifer as an example here to show you that, no matter how difficult your financial situation, you can be encouraged. By planning and setting goals on paper, you can see an end to those anxiety-producing money problems.

Jennifer has designed a budget and set some goals. Now it's your turn.

YOUR TURN

The first stage of budget-plotting is to determine approximate figures for your income and expenses during the past few months to a year.

Maybe you're saying, "Whoa! How do I come up with these figures? I can't remember what I spent on groceries last week, let alone for the last month." The most accurate method of determining your estimated expenses is to go back through your last year's checkbook and receipts.

This initial budget is based on what you now spend—not on your future hopes. Under income, write down all expected income for the year and divide it by twelve to get the average income per month. Some of your monthly expenses will be fixed and easy to find. Others, such as groceries and medical bills, will be more difficult. Go back through the past year and total all medical and dental bills. Find the monthly average.

If the thought of rummaging through a whole year's worth of bills just to come up with an estimate of one month's expenses has your blood pressure climbing, relax. Not all of the expenses need to be based on a full year. Telephone, utilities, insurance payments, taxes, and licenses should be figured that way because they may not be paid each month, or may vary greatly from month to month. As for groceries and clothing, you can venture a guess based on the previous three months.

Your final tallies should provide you with fairly accurate figures to place under the expense column of your monthly budget. Don't be surprised if the miscellaneous column scores high enough to win the title "Miscellaneous Money-Eater of the Year." Your budget, along with the spending reduction plans from the last three chapters, should soon have her ballooning figure down to size.

Now we're ready to insert the estimated income and expenses on the budget work sheets provided on pages 110-113 as a guide. On this sample budget plan, mark items that are pertinent to you with a yellow marker. Then go back and fill in the blanks. If you don't want to mark up the book, grab a pad and pencil and label four columns as illustrated.

1. *List all sources of expected income (see fig. 2).* If income varies, keep your estimate low.

Some of the experts I've read and talked with say you should include *all* income—interests, bonuses, dividends, and so on—in this budgeted income figure. However, unless these represent a significant proportion of your income, you may not want to list them. Then, when the extra cash comes in, slip it smugly into your savings account. It's always a thrill to receive an income that isn't already destined for the bill collectors.

Now that we've completed the easy and more enjoyable part of our budget, it's time to take a look at where our hard-earned money is spent.

2. *List all fixed expenses (see fig. 3).* These include obligations you must meet no matter what. Round off figures to the nearest ten.

3. *Subtract your total fixed expenses from your income.* Hopefully you will have money left over for the other necessities in life—such as food. Keep in mind one of the main principles in budgeting: If you overspend in one area, you must compensate by underspending in another.

4. *List all your variable expenses (see fig. 4).* These are items you need or want. They are termed "variable" because the amounts may vary from month to month and because variables are the items that are most often cut or trimmed when the money runs out. The following list of variables may or may not be a part of your life-style. Again, use a yellow marker to underline the items you will use in your budget.

5. *Subtract the variable expenses from the amount you have left over from paying the fixed expenses.* At this point in budget development, you may need someone beside you—a trusted friend who can assume one of two roles. One, she can help you celebrate—if you came out even or

ended up with a profit. Two, she can pick you off the floor or hand you a box of tissues if you ended up in the red.

How did you do? For those who came out on top, in the black or pink or whatever—congratulations! You are probably one of the few Americans who can claim success in living within your means. You have survived the deficit-spending bug. Deficit spending is catchy. Uncle Sam caught it years ago and has spread the disease around to citizens in epidemic proportions.

Unfortunately, while our great uncle can get away with operating in the red, we can't. Spending money you don't have can catch up with you and send you into bankruptcy.

GETTING OUT OF THE RED ZONE

If you find yourself operating in the red, don't panic. There are solutions. Ask Jennifer. Your first step is to get a cup of coffee or tea, put your feet up, and say to yourself, "I know that in Christ all things are possible. I can beat this." Ask God to show you ways to cut costs. When you're feeling better, grab your pencil and start trimming. Slice off dollars on those items that mean the least to you. Be ruthless.

We've already talked about ways of saving money on food, clothing, and household items. And you'll find some additional ways to save in chapter 9. Start from the bottom of the expense list and work up. One good thing about red is that it can be diluted down to pink. And "in the pink," as I understand it, is a cheery place to be.

To make you even more cheery, how about a simplified budget? Sound good? While some of the more complex money-makers and money-spenders will need a longer list of income and expense items, most of us can easily slip into this condensed version (see fig. 5).

WHY BUDGETS FAIL

Once you have cut your expenses and balanced them with your income, or come out with less expenses than income, you'll want to check it for leaks. The last thing we need is to have our budgets fail in the middle of the debt-infested sea.

The biggest mistake new budgeters make is to use their savings as compensation for overspending. The savings account is a must and serves as a cushion or buffer in emergencies. Or in our analogy, a sealant to plug the holes in our leaky budgets. A dwindled savings account could mean disaster if you suffer loss of income through job layoff, illness, accident, or death.

Monthly payments into a savings account can relieve the pressure of such an emergency. Most financial experts agree that our savings cushion should contain at least three months' wages. They also tell me it should be kept liquid, meaning cash that is readily available. Your liquid assets include checking accounts, passbook savings accounts, some money markets, and mutual funds.

No matter how desperate your budget cuts, keep that eraser away from savings.

FACING THE TRUTH

Many remain stuck in the money maze as a result of negative attitudes, false beliefs, and rationalizations. We tell ourselves lies in order to keep from feeling overwhelmed by seemingly unsolvable problems. These attitudes and beliefs affect us in many areas, including money management, weight control, substance abuse, sex, and relationships.

Let's take a moment to discover whether or not we are being hindered by a faulty belief system. Below are some

Lost in the Money Maze?

true and false statements. Use them to examine your feelings and values. In the space provided check under a "T" for a truth or reality statement, or an "F" to indicate a false belief or rationalization.

T F

[ ] [ ]   1. A budget is too restrictive.

[ ] [ ]   2. I work hard and deserve a treat regardless of what my budget dictates.

[ ] [ ]   3. I can give in just this once. It's not like I do it all the time.

[ ] [ ]   4. I'm just not talented in the area of budgeting and record keeping.

[ ] [ ]   5. If God expected me to keep records, he'd have given me a more highly developed left brain.

[ ] [ ]   6. I'm not good at balancing a checkbook or keeping records. It's just the way I am, so I may as well accept it.

[ ] [ ]   7. If you really need something, it's okay to go into debt for it.

[ ] [ ]   8. I can't follow a budget. I try but . . . I just can't.

[ ] [ ]   9. There are certain things a person can't resist. It's part of being human.

[ ] [ ] 10. I'm never going to get out of the money maze. It's too hard for me.

[ ] [ ] 11. If I really wanted to keep a budget I could.

[ ] [ ] 12. I'm the one who decides what I can and can't do.

[ ] [ ] 13. The truth is I'm a failure. I need to confess to God that I'm no good.

[ ] [ ] 14. I can do anything as long as it is God's will that I do it.

Answers: 1. F; 2. F; 3. F; 4. F; 5. F; 6. F; 7. F; 8. F; 9. F; 10. F; 11. T; 12. T; 13. F; 14. T.

As you can see, there are only three true statements in the above quiz. These truths can provide the strength we need to conquer false beliefs, rationalizations, and negative attitudes. We *can* keep a budget and maintain control over our finances. The choice is ours. When we seek God's will in overcoming our money problems, he provides strength for us to succeed.

IT'S ALL IN THE ATTITUDE

The success or failure of a budget depends largely on our attitude. As we recognize the lies we tell ourselves, our attitudes will change. We become possibility-thinkers instead of impossibility-thinkers. Rather than thinking of your budget as a prison, you'll see it as a vessel you designed to keep afloat financially. With it you know what you earn and spend. Your budget becomes a tool that helps you dispense your funds when and where you decide. Through a budget you can watch your savings grow and plan investments for the future. For those who now live in the storm-tossed sea of mismanagement and overspending, it can mean financial freedom.

In order to maintain a budget and live within the goals, you must think positively rather than negatively. Think *goal*, not limit. Think *plan*, not prison. Think *yes*, not no.

FINISH WHAT YOU START

Another thought I'd like to leave with you as we consider the importance of building a strong, seaworthy budget is the realization that God expects us to plan ahead. Jesus says, "For which of you, desiring to build a tower, does not first sit down and count the cost, whether he has enough to complete it? Otherwise, when he has laid a foundation and is not able to finish, all who see it begin to mock him."[1]

In other words it's foolish to start something you can't finish. If this principle applies to building a house, think how much more it should apply to developing plans that enhance the quality of our lives.

Besides faulty belief systems and failure to save, budgets fail due to:

1. *Family members who don't understand budgeting or won't cooperate.* (We'll talk more about this in the next chapter.)

2. *Overspending (credit card and loan abuse).*

3. *Impulse-buying.*

4. *Failure to live within one's means.*

It's not always easy to cut back on expenses. As we've seen before, sometimes we need to take a serious look at our priorities in life. If you are consistently living beyond your means, you may want to consider getting help from a consumer credit counseling service. This type of assistance is available throughout the U.S. For information check with a local library or your phone book.

Whether or not you need counseling, stay aboard. You won't want to miss these next two chapters as we set sail through a paper-sea toward the promised land of financial freedom.

TIME TO CONSIDER

1. Discuss the importance of budgeting with your partner or support group.

2. If you haven't worked with a budget, develop one this week using the work sheets provided.

3. Do your expenses exceed your income? If so, brainstorm about ways you can cut back.

4. Examine your heart attitude. Are you resentful about not having enough money to meet your expenses? Are you angry with God? Your husband? Yourself? Are you coveting what others have? Are you feeling anxious or overwhelmed? You may want to write your feelings in your diary or discuss them with your support person(s).

Pray together that God will help you prioritize and find ways to fit your expenses into the income he has allotted you. Ask his forgiveness for any anger, resentment, or jealousy you may have developed as well as for any overspending you have done.

As the Apostle Paul said in his letter to the Philippians, "Do not be anxious about anything, but in everything, by prayer and petition, with thanksgiving, present your requests to God. And the peace of God, which transcends all understanding, will guard your hearts and your minds in Christ Jesus."[2]

5. Trimming a budget requires wisdom in discerning priority items. It helps us to keep our focus on Christ and to love him above all things. Read John 21:15-17. Where the Bible says "Simon, son of John" substitute your own name. Listen to Jesus as he asks "_____, do you love me more than these?" Picture him pointing to the things you cherish most and give him an answer. This is a difficult task but one that helps us to keep a godly view.

BUDGET WORK SHEET—INCOME

ITEM	INCOME	EXPENSES	TOTAL
INCOME:			
Salary			
Salary—spouse			
Real estate income (rentals or contracts)			
Bonus/commission			
Dividends/interest income			
Pension/social security			
Other income			
TOTAL INCOME			

Figure 2

110

BUDGET WORK SHEET—FIXED EXPENSES

ITEM	INCOME	EXPENSES	TOTAL
Total income:			
FIXED EXPENSES:			
Tithe (10% of gross income or preference)			
Savings (5-10% of net income)			
Mortgage/rent			
a. Real estate taxes			
b. Home insurance			
Utilities (heat, electricity, water, garbage)			
Telephone			
Loans or installments (car, boat, home improvement)			
Income tax			
Health and life insurance			
Union dues			
Auto insurance			
Other			
TOTAL EXPENSES			
To total, subtract expenses from income			
Remaining funds for variable expenses			

Figure 3

Lost in the Money Maze?

BUDGET WORK SHEET—VARIABLE EXPENSES

ITEM	INCOME	EXPENSES	TOTAL
VARIABLE EXPENSES:			
Groceries (food and nonfood items, dining out)			
Household maintenance			
Clothing			
Clothing maintenance (cleaning/dry cleaning)			
Home furnishings and equipment			
Transportation (car repairs, gas and oil, commuting)			
Medical/dental			
Personal			
Child care/allowances			
Education			
Recreation			
Gifts/Christmas			
Recreation/vacation			
Miscellaneous			
To total, subtract expenses from "remaining funds for variable expenses"			-$
Total—over/short Expenses			$

Figure 4

SIMPLIFIED BUDGET PLAN

INCOME	
Salary—gross	
Interest/dividends	
Other income	
Total income	
EXPENSES	
Tithes/contributions	
Taxes	
Savings	
Rent/Mortgage	
Food	
Clothing	
Medical/dental	
Insurance	
Transportation	
Utilities/telephone	
Personal	
Entertainment/vacation	
Education	
Household purchases	
Miscellaneous	
Other	
Other	
Total expenses	
Balance over/short	

Figure 5

8

...

Budgeting–
a Family Affair

Budgeting—unless you're single and without kids—should involve the whole family. By being involved, I don't mean that one of you earns the money and the others spend it. What I do mean is that, ideally, every family member should learn to earn, save, spend, budget, and invest.

Whether you flounder through the financial worries alone or with a spouse, if you have children, you'll want to get them in on the act as well. Later in this chapter, we'll talk about training the kids to handle money—yours and theirs. But first, let's look at the married group and the budget battles that so often flare up between husbands and wives.

SHARING THE LOAD

Who wears the financial pants in your family? In many homes budgeting and bookkeeping fall to one person. In

115

the earlier years of our marriage, even though we both worked outside the home, I landed the job of chief accountant. While my husband made investments, I was responsible for budgets, bills, check statements, and bookkeeping. Even though I had the credentials, at times, the job seemed overwhelming.

A few years ago, I made my plea for equality and suggested Ron take over a larger share and that we work together for a more peaceful coexistence. You see, we had taken to arguing over who spent what, why, and how much. The tension of my unawareness of his investment ventures and his unawareness of how much it actually cost to run a household often left us both short—short-tempered and short of cash. By working together, we could understand each other's problems. Eventually, instead of "*you* are spending too much money," it became, "*we* are spending too much." With the reconciliation, we not only negotiate the budget, but we share the load.

On the other hand, some women have told me that their husbands insist on doing *all* the budgeting, bookkeeping, and investing. The wives are given an allowance for household expenses. If this is your situation and you're happy with the arrangement, you don't need to change. Remember, though, for both your sakes, you should know all the facets of your family's money management program in case you end up on your own.

But are you really happy? Maybe you'd like to play a more significant role in the family's finances, but you think your husband would laugh.

"My husband," Kathy declared, "would say, 'You can't even handle the grocery budget. How do you expect me to turn you loose on mine?'

"Maybe he's right." She sighed. "For years every time he mentioned balancing the budget, the stock market, or investment securities, I threw my mind into automatic pilot. My mouth released an occasional 'Uh-huh, hmmm, oh, that's nice, Dear.' I couldn't shift gears until the conversation came back to a more common ground like, 'What's for dinner?' "

I can understand Kathy's hesitation. Let's face it. A woman who has spent the last few years of her life rinsing diapers, wiping noses, and learning that "goo-doo-ba-dibby-dow" means food, will have a rough time transitioning into the sophisticated world of finance. It's hard for a man to take his wife's interest in money seriously when she's been more concerned with the pabulum running down Baby's chin than with their money matters.

You can show your husband you are genuinely interested in several ways. First, ask him how you can help keep the budget under control. Offer to balance the checkbook and pay the bills. Remember, though, your goal is to share, not to have the whole load dumped on you so he can get in a few more hours of leisure time. While we'd all—husbands and wives—like to escape the woes of managing money, it's a big load for one. Unfortunately, the person in charge all too often finds himself or herself in the role of the villain or dictator. Decisions about how money is disbursed lose their sting when made by family consensus.

If you and your husband have decided to team up and share the load, we'll need to talk about some goals and game rules.

TEAMWORK

Your first step in working together as a team is to set goals. Maybe your first priority is to create a budget you can both live with. Other goals may be to save for a house or vacation. Your concerns may be as simple as having enough money left from your paycheck for groceries. Be sure to set realistic goals for yourselves in order to avoid discouragement. By extending your marriage contract to include the better and worse of money matters you tie a more secure knot.

Be certain to allow room in your budget for those "little things" that help nurture your relationship. Special dinners out, gifts, and time-out trips keep both the romantic and financial side of your marriage running smoothly.

Partnership budgeting and money management require that you both know the entire financial picture. You don't necessarily have to trade jobs every other month, in fact, in many cases that is impractical. However, you should each take the time to study every facet.

To help you decide who does what, list the money-related jobs facing your family during the year—budgeting, bookkeeping, balancing the checkbook, paying bills, and so on. Take turns choosing one, then another, until they are all taken. Remember, budgeting, regardless of who got the job of recording, is a joint venture. Sit down as a team to plan it.

The key to teamwork is flexibility. In the trade-off system you have the security of knowing neither your home nor its financial state of affairs will collapse if one of the partners takes a leave of absence.

Whether you choose to keep the same jobs all the time or to trade doesn't matter. What is more important than trading is to be open to each other's problems and needs. Be understanding and develop a spirit of giving.

Yes, I said to develop a spirit of giving. Selfishness has done more to trigger the battle of the budget than any other cause.

Suppose Jenny wants a new dress this month, and Jim declares his desire for a new set of golf clubs. Their slim budget can't handle both requests. What do they do?

First, find out exactly how much money can be allotted to these extra items. Then, determine a need. Can Jim live without his new clubs? Will Jenny suffer undue humility by having nothing to wear? Next, come to a mutual agreement. If neither can agree, bring up the subject again next month. Do not stubbornly stomp off to the mall and charge it. Your budget will suffer for months and so will your marriage. Think it through and ask yourself, *is it worth it?* Finally, avoid the whole issue by establishing priorities and setting others' needs above your own.

Now, whether you are a single parent or are happily co-budgeting with your spouse, it's time to bring in the kids.

MONEY MATTERS TO KIDS, TOO

"Bring in the kids?" you may stammer. "It's too late. My teenage son thinks a budget is something too heavy to move. My daughter tells me financial freedom is owning her own credit card—in my name."

Ideally, parents set an example of good money management and include their children in the family financial responsibilities at an early age. Unfortunately, most parents miss the ideal and find themselves caught in the revolving credit door of life. Perhaps you are just now in the process of overcoming years of impulse-buying and overspending. You nearly lost your head with a case of the credit-card crazies. Now you're coming to your senses.

Spending withdrawals hit you only once every couple of months, and you can feel the money-hungry habits dropping off your back. The handle you could never get hold of hovers just within your grasp.

If you're in the process of piecing your financial life back together again, I can understand why you might feel it's too late to teach your children well—but it's not. That is, unless your kids have left home. Even then, you may

119

still have a chance to provide wise financial counsel. There's nothing like the testimony of someone who's nearly drowned in an ocean of debts to help keep someone else from making the same mistakes.

For those kids still in the nest, start now. Sit down with them and explain the financial facts of life. Perhaps they will rebel at the changes; it's a chance you have to take. But let's hope your children are understanding and accept the new, budget-wise you.

Include the children in your family budgeting sessions as early as possible. While you can't expect four-year-old Michael to fill you in on his profit-and-loss statement for the current fiscal year, he can give you a few pointers on his special needs and where he'd like to vacation this summer.

Even though you can include children in your budget planning to a small extent, they will have to reach the age of reason before you can expect them to understand how the budget works. We decided our son had reached that magic age when he turned eight.

"Mom!" my son's voice echoed up from behind the radio counter at Sears. "Mom, come quick. Ya gotta see this. It's a radio with a digital clock and snooze alarm so's you won't haf'ta wake me up in the morning. And see, it's covered with fur so's I can sleep with it. Can I have it?"

As my fingers fumbled with the price tag, my tongue became dry and I shifted nervously. "I'm sorry, Honey, but I don't have enough money and your allowance couldn't possibly . . ."

"Ah, Mom, it's only seventy-six dollars, and it's on sale. I could pay a dollar a month."

"No, I'm afraid not. You're too young for a loan. You don't have any collateral . . ."

My words drifted over his head. "Mom," he brightened, "you don't need any money—just charge it."

His statement washed over me like fog. What had I taught my kids? Or maybe I should say, what *hadn't* I taught them?

THE FINANCIAL FACTS OF LIFE

I knew it was time to sit down to a father-mother-son talk about the financial facts of life. We'd avoided the subject long enough. It was time to bring matters out in the open.

We talked about checks and how intimately they were related to the amount of money you had in the bank. We told him the bitter truth about lending, and how you shouldn't indulge in credit-card buying unless you were willing to face your responsibilities afterward.

"You always end up paying for your transactions," we cautioned him.

Letting Dave in on our financial secrets wasn't easy. Once we did, we had no guarantee he wouldn't leak classified information into the neighborhood. I relaxed a little when I realized that our profit-and-loss statement or J.C. Penney bill was not a priority subject in the neighborhood war games, space cadets, and marbles tournaments.

I'm certain you, too, will feel relief as you step forward and explain financial facts to your children. Once you've explained that money doesn't grow on trees just like they didn't arrive by stork, you'll feel a sense of satisfaction. Truth releases the guilt parents feel over those gray areas we somehow can't quite bring ourselves to confess. Discussing finances can make you feel good about your communication skills as a parent. Who knows, next year you may even disclose the facts about Santa Claus.

When you tell your children about budgets and how to earn and spend money wisely, take it slow. Don't stuff their brains with too much information too quickly. Remember, you're not going to turn your six-year-old into a financial genius in an hour. Be fair. Don't expect to turn the budget over to the kids for at least a month.

BEGIN WITH LOGICAL CONSEQUENCES

Kim used logical consequences to teach her son his first lesson in finances.

"Mom," called six-year-old Ben. "I need some more allowance. Mine's all runned out."

"No, Ben," Kim explained, "Daddy and I told you your allowance had to last a week."

"Ya, but I spent it, so you gotta gimme some more."

"I'm sorry, Honey . . ." Kim began.

"Com'on, Mom," Ben pleaded. "Bret's mom's gonna take us roller skating an' I need fifty cents."

"Ben," Kim asked. "How much money did you have yesterday?"

"A dollar and a half." Ben beamed.

"And what happened to all that money?"

"I told you I spent it. I got candy and pop and a Match Box truck and . . . stuff."

Kim sighed. "And now you don't have any money for skating. That's too bad. I guess you'll have to stay home."

Ben stared at his mother as tears of unbelief trickled down his face.

What a tough lesson. And what better way to teach that all important truth: You can't spend what you don't have.

ALLOWANCES

Allowances teach. Or, at least they can, providing you link up the allowance with job responsibility and a budget. A question parents most commonly ask concerning allowances is, "At what age should allowances start?"

If your child seems to have an accurate idea of what

money will buy, try a small allowance. Most children six years and older will enjoy handling their own spending money. However, some youngsters, like Annie, may appreciate a different type of reward system.

When Annie's mother heard her offer to a neighborhood friend, she decided an allowance could wait. "I'll trade you a zillion pennies if I can have two stars and a rainbow sticker," Annie bargained.

"Well, okay," came the reluctant reply.

Rather than give Annie a money allowance, Mom chose to reward her with stars and stickers for jobs well-done. At the end of each week or month, the stars and stickers are counted and given a monetary value. Under this system Annie can save for a special doll or cash in on an occasional treat.

While Annie may be happy with stars and stickers, other six-year-olds may want to enter the world of high finance. Use your intuition to determine whether your youngsters are ready for allowances.

Once you've determined your child should receive an allowance, you'll probably wonder, *How much should we give?*

Base your youngster's allowance on needs, living expenses, and outside jobs. Consider, also, your particular life-style. Be realistic. If you expect eight-year-old Debbie to pay for all her entertainment, books, magazines, hobbies, sports equipment, school activities, lunches, expenses, gifts, and contributions, she'll need more than a dollar a week.

Sit down with your child and draw up a list of expenses and needs. Then come to terms on an income. You will probably want to correlate allowance to job responsibilities.

If you want to start giving your children their financial wings, let them manage their own money. Not sure where to start? The following guidelines may help you decide what expenses your kids can handle. By the way, money for these expenses comes from allowance plus wages, depending on capabilities.

• Ages seven and younger: crayons, books, small toys, candy, gum, gifts for their friends, contributions, and savings.

• Ages seven to ten: entertainment, toys, books, magazines, hobbies, school expenses such as games, sports, lunches, supplies, social events, sports equipment, gifts, contributions, and savings.

• Ages ten to thirteen: all of the above, plus clothing and upkeep. (For kids ages ten and older, whenever possible, the allowance should decrease and outside earnings increase.)

• Ages thirteen and older: the above plus personal items for grooming, hair care, cosmetics, transportation expenses including auto, gas, insurance, license fees, traffic tickets, and possibly part of their vacation expenses.

"Wait," you may be saying, "my ten-year-old can't even remember to take a bath. How can I expect him to budget for school supplies, lunch, and other items you so casually mentioned?"

While the list of expenses may seem unrealistic for some children, others, like Lisa, who is eight-going-on-twenty, will find it ideal.

As I mentioned, don't expect allowances to cover all the expenses, especially once your youngsters hit ten. Allow what you can, and expect them to work at additional jobs for the rest.

If they can't think of a thing to do, I'm sure you have a few ideas of your own. How about grooming the neighbor's dog—or yard, washing cars, selling iced drinks on a hot summer day. Should you run short of brainstorms, Malcolm

124

MacGregor's book *Training Your Children to Handle Money* has more money making schemes than the U.S. Patent Office. The book will also give you additional advice on teaching your child the art of money management.

IF YOU DON'T WORK, YOU DON'T EAT

One of the most frequently asked questions about allowances is: "Should the allowance be related to household chores?" Years ago, a child psychologist convinced me that I should give my children an allowance to cover their needs with no strings attached. My children, filled with thankfulness, compassion, and cheerful hearts, would then diligently complete their fair share of the cleaning.

This psychologist obviously had never met a real child. The system wasn't working. When I told my charming youngsters they had to help with household chores because they lived here and were expected to do their share, they threatened to move in with Grandma. The idea of an allowance to meet needs and working for nothing didn't suit my philosophy. After all, in the real world we get paid according to our job performance.

I wasn't sure how to facilitate the change. By paying the kids for every task performed, I'd risk losing my sanity. Can you imagine one of your money-hungry little tyrants dusting the television set four times a day, demanding payment each time? Likewise, I would not expect to pay a child for cleaning his or her own room.

The obvious solution for our family fell easily into place. We would use a combination of chores without pay and jobs with earning power. Expected household chores without pay included making beds and cleaning rooms, some laundry, and a fair share of dishes and garbage duties.

All other chores, chosen on ability, were assigned. Allowances were based on these jobs. Additional money could be earned by washing windows, cleaning the car, mowing lawns, and so on.

Whatever job responsibilities you attach to allowances, you'll need to take some time out of your busy schedule each week to evaluate job performance and ability to budget. Is Kenny dusting the furniture every week? Did Susy clean the three-month supply of laundry out from under her bed? Does the bathroom tell tales of a fresh cleaning with Pine-Sol or would your guest wonder if you've ever heard of indoor plumbing? Has your cat threatened to find another owner unless you change her litter box?

Although we'd like to put our children on the honor system, it's not practical. We all need periodic evaluations. Evaluations should also be made on the youngster's ability to budget. The budget you drew up to determine how much allowance to give will make a good beginning. Ask your child to write down all expenses each week. Keeping records at this early age will not only help the child live within a budget now, but will, hopefully, become a habit in adulthood.

Keep your child's budget, allowance, and spending experience real. In other words, if Tommy blew his wad at the ice cream parlor on Monday and has no money for the rest of the week's expenses, what do you do?

You could bail him out, but would that keep him from repeating his actions? Would the local banker have that kind of mercy on you? Hardly. You may wish to advance Tommy some of next week's allowance, but he needs to undergo a hardship for his impulsive mistake. Be firm but understanding.

Your goals with allowances are to give your children a

taste of the real world of finances and to wean them from dependence to independence.

TEACH BY EXAMPLE

You teach your child budget-wise living by example. For instance, while you push your grocery cart down the aisles, think aloud. "Hmmm," you may mutter, "turtle eggs have gone up to almost three dollars a dozen. Maybe I should substitute chicken eggs. I'd save $1.50."

Or, maybe Johnnie is begging for Fruitie Lutties, the "out-of-orbit" breakfast treat. It promises a galaxy of little stars, planets, rocket ships, and astronauts in bite-sized chunks, already sugar-coated and dipped in fluoride to guard against cavities.

"Look, Johnnie," you explain, as you price it against Heroes, the whole wheat flakes that keep hula-hoopers from losing their pep halfway through competition. "Fruitie Lutties cost $1.39 more than Heroes. We'll buy Heroes and you can tell Daddy how much money we saved."

Little Johnnie will not be impressed. In fact, you'll be lucky if he stops wailing by the time you get to the checkout stand. But, hopefully, he permanently recorded your example in his subconscious for future reference.

It *does* work. Our son Dave, at thirteen, came home with a super bargain. He'd been wanting a guitar. By comparison shopping, we found we could get a beginner for about fifty dollars. He had just started saving for it when he chanced upon a neighborhood garage sale. A "hardly used" guitar beckoned him from its lonely corner and displayed a price of fifteen dollars. David, having been taught comparison shopping and negotiating, offered ten dollars. "It's all I've got," he said. The seller agreed. What a buy. It carried him through two years of lessons and moved on to our daughter.

"Train a child in the way he should go, and when he is old he will not turn from it" (Prov. 22:6). This well-worn proverb has mostly been used in books on rearing well-behaved kids. Money management is an area that should receive as much importance as behavioral management. Both areas need discipline. When we come down to basics, that is what budgeting is—discipline.

You and I will probably agree that it is much harder to discipline yourself in adulthood if you were not taught the art as a child. So do your children a favor. Train them up in the way they should go—toward wisdom and discipline in money management.

MORE BUDGETING POINTERS

Along with allowances and examples, I'd like to make a few additional points about family budgeting.

1. *Show the kids the give-and-take philosophy of a budget.* For example, money for the extras like a vacation to Hawaii may be saved by not eating for a month. Or, they can take part in cutting out snacks; offering a percentage of their allowance; more frugal use of electricity, school paper, and supplies; spending less on clothing; and so on.

Likewise, if your clothes-crazy Carla wants to spend forty dollars on a designer shirt, she'll have to give up some of the less important items in her budget such as the championship football game, the ski trip to Mount Bachelor, or the senior prom.

2. *Don't argue over money, and don't blame your spending habits on the kids.* One ulcer in the family is enough. Perhaps the kids *are* a strain on the budget, but it's not their fault. Sudden and continuous growth spurts make it hard to keep them in clothes, and food bills soar in the presence of growing teenage boys. Bickering over who unbalanced the budget won't solve the problem.

128

3. *Taking part in the goals and planning of the family budget gives children a feeling of importance.* Self-esteem builds as they see their opinions and suggestions listened to, weighed, discussed, and sometimes used. Family budgeting can build family unity.

4. *Get your older children in on the action of record keeping.* The partnership program could easily include your teenager. A turn at keeping records and working with a family budget gives the youngster a look at what he or she will face in the future.

Dale and Edna came up with an interesting answer for their demanding teenager.

"Why can't we buy the Olson's sailboat, Dad? It's only thirty thousand dollars," sixteen-year-old Todd grumbled. "Everybody's got one but us."

"The Olson's won't after they sell theirs."

"That's different. Mr. Olson lost his job and they can't make the payments. Besides," Todd added, "you've got money."

"I'll tell you what, Son," Dale calmly approached his son. "Here is my paycheck, the checkbook, the bills, and the budget. You figure it all out for the next couple of months. Write the checks and I'll sign them. If you can come up with a better way of handling the money, fine. See if you can squeeze payments for a sailboat out of it."

"Wow! Thanks, Dad," exclaimed the confident lad.

Excellent experience for a teen, don't you think? Interestingly enough, the subject of the sailboat mysteriously sank under the reality of keeping the budget afloat.

Money matters to kids. Whether you teach purposefully or choose to ignore the subject, they will learn. They will either learn the art of spending frivolously and foolishly or prudently with discernment. You set the example; the choice is yours.

TIME TO CONSIDER

1. If you are married, what is your current financial role? Is the work balanced?

2. Discuss with your partner or support group the pros and cons of sharing the load. What does Ecclesiastes 4:9-12 say to us regarding this?

3. Write down the changes you'd like to make in your own situation, and choose one or two as your goal before the next meeting.

4. Evaluate your present situation in involving the children in your money matters. What, if anything, would you like to change? Again make a list and choose reachable goals that you can attain within a specific time period.

9
...

Climbing Paper
Mountains

We no sooner cross our ocean of debt when another deterrent crosses our path—a mountain of paperwork. This has been my greatest challenge in navigating the money maze. Every year I resolved to keep better records. And every year, tax time found me in a puddle of tears as I sorted through stacks of receipts I'd tossed in a drawer.

Tax time is still a chore, but I'm happy to say that the trauma and the tears are a thing of the past. Not because I've become a fantastically organized bookkeeper, but because I've come to accept my personality and chosen a record-keeping system tailored for me.

I encourage you to do the same. In the next few pages we'll talk about the whys of record keeping, then we'll begin with the most basic record-keeping method and work our way up.

WHY KEEP RECORDS?

Obviously, records help you keep track of your financial situation or condition. But a more important reason for records is Uncle Sam. The government induces us to record income and expenses so they can collect their fair share.

We also keep records to account for our expenditures. This is especially true if you maintain a checking account. Bankers frown on the practice of writing checks on a zero or minus balance. Besides, it's illegal.

Along with keeping you out of jail, records can keep you out of the poorhouse. It is a well-known fact that careful record keeping can reduce the risk of overspending and help you maintain your leak-proof budget.

How you choose to keep those records is entirely up to you. We all have varied life-styles, personalities, and incomes. Naturally, some will want to keep more detailed records than others. So, let's get on with finding a method just for you.

THE TOSS-IT-IN-A-DRAWER-TILL-TAX-TIME TECHNIQUE

I've started with the simplest, most basic system. It's the one I call toss-it-in-a-drawer-till-tax-time. This is dedicated to people, like Janet, who believe numbers were created for the sole purpose of confusing them.

It also serves as a great system for busy women who haven't discovered that "Superwoman" is a myth. The toss-it technique works but only on the items that can be put on hold for a year at a time. Even with this most simplified method, you can't escape the monthly bill-paying and checkbook duties.

Here is how it works:

1. *Reserve a drawer or file folder.* In it, toss all the

132

receipts collected during the year for tax purposes. This includes paycheck stubs, completed bank statements with canceled checks, cash and charge receipts.

2. *At the year's end, haul out your stuffed drawer or file and dump it on the floor or table.*

3. *Begin the sorting process.* For most households, the job should take about four hours. More complex households, however, with small businesses, rental properties, or other investments may find this sort-and-record session lasting up to four days. To simplify the job, file the receipts in an accordion file folder or in envelopes.

4. *Total, clip, and staple the receipts from each category and record the title and total on top for easy reading.*

5. *Record your totals on a work sheet.*

6. *Give yourself a standing ovation.*

7. *Call your tax preparer for an appointment.* Or, if you're up to the challenge, do it yourself.

The toss-it style is a workable method—if you can handle the big job of sorting and filing every year. The secret of successful "toss-iters" is acceptance. Accept the fact that this technique is your choice. You have exchanged small increments of time during the year for one lump sum at the end.

Approach it in a cheerful, matter-of-fact manner. You may want to begin positive-mind preparation as early as October or November. Repeat phrases like "I'm really looking forward to sitting down with that pile of papers." Positive statements repeated often enough might actually make you believe what you say.

THE ONCE-A-MONTH METHOD

Suppose the toss-it idea, no matter how much you enjoy that year-long freedom from records, leaves you feeling unfulfilled and irritated come January. Maybe, no matter how hard you tried, you couldn't find happiness with a year's worth of bookkeeping to do at one time. If you'd really like to get a firmer grip on your paperwork, here's an idea that might let you continue your drawer-stuffing technique and minimize the January workload.

Since you are bound by your bill collectors to slip into the role of bill-payer and bank-statement-balancer once a month, why not follow my friend Martha's example? Use that time more efficiently. Add half an hour to your task.

Wait! Before you tell me your time budget has been stretched too far already, read on. You're sitting at a desk or table anyway, right? After you pay the bills and come to an agreement with the bank's computer over your checkbook, open the infamous receipt drawer. By the way, if you start this new system in January, you won't have to make up lost time.

1. *Label envelopes or file folders with Income, Mortgage, Telephone, Utilities, and so on.* (Use the item list from your budget form in chapter 7.) You may want to include nondeductible items such as groceries and clothing to help you with your budget totals.

2. *Place all canceled checks, statements, and other receipts into the corresponding folders.*

3. *File your receipts at the same time you pay bills and do your check statement.* Once the initial files are set up, filing the receipts each month takes only minutes.

If you don't own a file cabinet and can't afford one, a pre-labeled, accordion-type file folder or even a sturdy shoe box will suffice. A variety store near me has one called the 21-Pocket Data File for about seven dollars.

By giving up an extra few minutes a month, you'll eliminate the troublesome task of transforming a pile of papers into an identifiable list of income and deductions in January. All of your receipts will be in presorted categories, and all you'll have to do is run totals, record them on a work sheet, and they're ready for the tax forms.

At tax time, tally all deductible expenses and list them neatly on a columnar pad headed: *Tax Records*. It's so neat, Martha's tax person sends her flowers (see fig. 6).

LEDGERS, JOURNALS, AND DIARIES

Don't let the titles turn you away. It's not that difficult. In fact, Martha's tax record is a simple ledger. I'm going to teach you a basic home-bookkeeping system, and you can build it up any way you choose. This is for persons who find their record keeping requirements have become more than what toss-it-in-a-drawer-till-tax-time or the once-a-month method can offer.

Many of you have jobs away from home or are involved with your own businesses. Perhaps you need or prefer monthly totals of your expenses. If so, that's where ledgers, journals, and diaries come in.

A ledger or journal refers to a columnar, ruled paper onto which you transfer your receipts of income and expenses. The work sheet you prepared for budgeting was, in fact, an unrefined journal. With ledgers and journals, you reap the benefits of a one- or two-page account of expenses and income instead of a drawer or file full of receipts.

Let's begin with a ledger—a simple two-column sheet on which we keep records of single accounts. Say, for example, you wanted to keep a separate account of your expenditures. Your ledger sheet for clothing might look like this (see fig. 7).

The ledger is an excellent way to keep track of cash allowances. In other words, if you draw two hundred dollars every two weeks to cover groceries, a ledger helps you keep close account of your income and expenses.

135

Lost in the Money Maze?

A journal can save you time with year-end tax records if you add a smidgen more time to your bookkeeping job each month. It also helps you with your budgeting. In fact, I've mapped out a simple journal that tells you at the end of the month whether or not you over- or underspent your income. (As if you needed proof.) This journal is called a cash disbursement journal, which is just a fancy name for cash in, cash out (see fig. 8).

You can buy journals already headed or use do-it-yourself columnar pads. I prefer the columnar pads, so I can choose my own headings.

My appointment book/diary proves its value every day. I use it to enter mileage and business meals, as well as other miscellaneous expenses. It serves as a ledger as well as tells me where I'm going and where I've been. And believe me, some days my brain can use the extra help. See figure 9 for a sample of my diary.

YOUR COMPUTER

The computer—high-technology style of record keeping—fits a wide variety of personalities. A number of software programs are available for home and business financial management. Some programs budget, balance checkbooks, pay bills, and fill out tax forms. They can even plan menus and create corresponding grocery lists. About the only thing a computer doesn't do is repair a broken budget.

Computers are wonderful—as long as you stay current and back up your disks.

Kathy bought a home computer. "It's wonderful. Besides helping me keep perfect records, the games entertain the kids for hours."

Unfortunately, as Kathy discovered, computers do have their limitations. Last December an ice storm knocked out power all over east Vancouver. Kathy's computer lost its memory—and she had forgotten to make backups. A year's worth of budgets, balances, and bills paid disappeared as her IBM popped, wheezed, and died.

Fortunately, before her home computer days, Kathy had perfected the toss-it technique. Her . . . ah . . . filing system paid off. As a matter of habit, she routinely tossed receipts in box on her file cabinet. All she had to do was sort through them.

TAX RECORDS—WHAT TO KEEP

You are legally bound by the government to document all income. This includes:

• Salary (total wages, federal tax withheld, FICA, state, and local taxes. Most of this information should appear on your W-2 form, which your employer should mail to you no later than January 31.)

• Alimony received (excluding child support)
• Interest and dividend income
• Income from sale of property, stocks, mutual funds, etc.
• Royalties, commissions, and fees
• Bonuses and prizes
• Tips and gratuities
• Annuities and pension income
• Lump sum distribution from retirement plans
• Unemployment compensation
• Social Security benefits
• Veteran's benefits
• Workers' compensation
• Other income: _____

With most of the above you will be given a statement or W-2 form. File them. With others, such as tips, keep a daily record or diary.

Lost in the Money Maze?

Because of individual qualifications and changing laws, you'll need to pick up the latest IRS tax guide.

Keeping track of these expenses and deductions isn't the overwhelming job it may seem. Simply keep in a file, or a drawer if you wish, all the canceled checks, paid invoices, receipts, or other papers that show your income and deductible expenses. You will need to keep these records and receipts for seven years after the due date for filing your income tax in case you are audited.

Because of the complexity of filling out tax forms, many choose to file the EZ 1040 short tax form.

WHO SHOULD DO YOUR TAXES?

Once you know what the IRS requires for filing tax forms, it's time to consider who will fill out the forms. Maybe you are thinking about saving money and doing them yourself. If you are filing the simple form and can read IRS jargon, you should have no problem.

However, if your earning and spending situation require the long form, you may want help. Doing my own taxes thrills me about as much as eating worms.

Why? Well, for one thing, it takes years of training to develop an aptitude for the technicalities of our tax system. In addition, the laws are constantly changing. The last time we had our taxes done, our accountant took out three different notebooks, each four inches thick, to help us decide how to fill out the forms to our best tax advantage. I have neither the time nor the desire to do my own taxes.

If you choose a CPA or a tax preparer, find one you can trust and one who will work in your best interests. Remember that even though someone else may fill out your tax forms, you are the one responsible for getting the right information to your agent. Have your papers in order by using one of the bookkeeping systems provided for you in

138

this chapter. It will save you and your agent time, and save you money.

Should you decide you like a challenge and you don't think the IRS will dispute you, do your own taxes. Obtain *Your Federal Income Tax* from your local IRS office. With some intense study and concentration you can pull it off. Good luck!

Conquering a mountain of paper work seldom falls into the thrill-a-minute category. Yet scripture tells us to "count it all joy . . . when you meet with various trials."[1] I don't know about you, but after all that sorting, recording, filing, and counting I'm more tearful than joyful. You, too?

Not to worry. We'll find our joy as we make our way past the now neatly stacked rows of paper into the final phase of our financial journey. Join me as we face our final obstacle in the money maze and discover the secrets of financial freedom.

Ahhh! We're smiling already.

TIME TO CONSIDER

1. How is your record keeping coming? Do you see how accurate record keeping can help you maintain your budget? Do you need to revise your system?

2. Which style of bookkeeping most closely fits your personality style?

3. What has record keeping to do with God? How can I please God in terms of my attitude and responsibilities?

4. Now is a good time to reflect on your journey through the money maze. How far have you come? Which money-eaters have you tamed? Which obstacles do you still need to work on?

5. Make a list of the small steps or goals you've accomplished.

6. Sometimes when we find ourselves making little or no progress or not moving fast enough we tend to let discouragement trample us underfoot. Take a moment and meditate on Philippians 1:6, "Being confident of this, that he who began a good work in you will carry it on to completion until the day of Christ Jesus . . ."

TAX RECORDS

ITEM	INCOME	EXPENSE
Salary: Jim	$14,440.00	
Ora (see W-2 forms)	6,000.00	
Interest income: First Federal	143.80	
Pacific First Federal	368.39	
Expenses: Medical		$267.30
Dental		342.00
Contributions		340.00
Union dues		300.00
Uniforms—Nursing		126.88
5/18 Casualty loss— 1972 Toyota, net loss		750.00

Figure 6

ADDRESS CLOTHING		NAME BUDGETED AMOUNT $80.00									
MEMO		TERMS			LIMIT		ACCOUNT NO.		SHEET NO.		
DATE		ITEM	FOL			BUDGET		EXPENSES		BALANCE	
Jan	1	Balance Forward								42	00
		Budget for January				80	00			122	00
		Mervyns—swimsuit						15	00	107	00
	15	J.C. Penneys—nylons						4	50	102	50
	15	Nordstrom—dress						46	00	56	50
		CY's House of Samples— misc.						42	00	14	50
		Totals				80	00	107	50	14	50
Feb	1	Balance Forward								14	50
		Budget for February				80	00				

Figure 7

MONTHLY CASH DISBURSEMENT JOURNAL—
January

	wk #1	wk #2	wk #3	wk #4	**Monthly Totals**
Tithes, contributions	$ 60.00	$ 60.00	$ 60.00	$ 60.00	$ 240.00
Savings	25.00	75.00			100.00
Mortgage	250.00		200.00		450.00
Utilities		30.00			30.00
Telephone			18.00		18.00
Food				300.00	300.00
Clothing			35.00		35.00
Insurance			38.00		38.00
Transportation	28.00	65.00	32.00	28.00	153.00
Medical/Dental				45.00	45.00
Personal/Entertainment	12.00				12.00
Education					
Miscellaneous		(Taxes)	60.00		
TOTAL EXPENSES	$375.00	$230.00	$443.00	$433.00	$1421.00
A) Salary	500.00		500.00	500.00	1500.00
B) Rental Income		350.00			350.00
TOTAL INCOME	$500.00	$350.00	500.00	$500.00	$1850.00
MINUS TOT'L EXP.	375.00	230.00	443.00	433.00	1421.00
TOTAL BALANCE	$125.00	$120.00	$ 57.00	$ 67.00	$ 429.00

Figure 8

Monday, March 7

66th Day — 299 days to follow

10:00am Bible Study

11:30am Lunch
Interview w/ Sharon
@ Marshall House
Re: books / records
cost of lunch: $11.38
mileage: 35
work: 6-11

Figure 9

143

10

...

Finding Financial Freedom

Financial freedom! Has a nice ring to it, don't you think? What does *financial freedom* mean to you?

For Janet it means "getting out from under all these bills."

"If I were financially free, I could go anywhere, buy anything, and never worry about overspending," said Sarah.

"To me," Jill said, "financial freedom means security. Having enough money to live comfortably for the rest of my life."

According to Karen, "It's never having money problems."

These were among the most common answers I received when I asked the question, "What is financial freedom?"

Most of these definitions refer to the dependency on money to supply various wants and needs. Most people feel that enough money would solve their financial problems, reduce stress, give security, and produce a happy life.

True financial freedom is what we find when we successfully navigate the money maze. And we've come a long way in overcoming the obstacles. After all, we've outmaneuvered the nibbling mice, managed to control that ferocious money-eating dragon, Charge, and crossed the Ocean of Debt with a sturdy, leak-proof budget. And finally, we've conquered our paper mountain by developing a usable record-keeping system. Surely now our way will be clear.

As we follow a little-used path we come to a small stone cell. A brilliant light shines through a doorway at the top of a concrete stairway. The good news is: All we have to do is climb three steps. The bad news is: Each step is six feet high.

PROVIDE AND CONQUER

The first step you must reach in exiting the money maze lifts you from your debts and grants you limited freedom from money worries. In order to reach this plateau you must be able to provide necessities, such as food, clothing, and shelter, for yourselves and your family. To reach your first step you should be able to answer yes to the following questions.

1. *Does your present income provide for your family's needs?* (Not wants, but *needs*.)

2. *Do you have a small store of extra food, water, and fuel in case of a crisis?*

3. *Do you have three to six months' worth of your income (minus taxes) in a secure and liquid, or easily accessible, savings account in case of an emergency?*

4. *Do you have adequate life, medical, and home insurance?*

5. *Have you set up a retirement fund?*

How did you do? Many people never reach this level in their money maze. Yet the completion of this phase is necessary if we want to avoid the pitfalls of worry and anxiety over financial affairs. Once we have established these priorities, we can advance to the second step—investing.

INVEST AND GROW

If we learn to live within our budgets and save regularly, we may find that we are ready to invest our extra money.

Perhaps your first investment will be to buy U.S. savings bonds, money market funds, certificates of deposit, or treasury bills. You may, after you've saved twenty percent for a down payment, want to invest in a home or other property. Some investors say mutual funds are highly recommended for this growing area. Be aware that, although many of these investments offer growth, there is always a potential risk.

God is not against our taking risks, even when it comes to money. The parable of the talents in Matthew 25:14-30 tells us that. When the servants doubled their money, the Master was pleased.

How would God have reacted if the servants had invested the whole bundle and lost their tunics? I'd like to think that if they had invested as wisely and prayerfully as they knew how, and still failed, the Master would have quickly forgiven them.

I suspect that God wants us to exercise caution in our investments. After all, we're taking risks with his money. Prayer, study, and a thorough investigation can help us reduce risks and should be a prerequisite for heading into any type of investment. Successfully managing this step takes time and effort to learn about the best and safest ways to invest what you have so that you, too, can be a "good and faithful servant."

Once you've made provisions for your family and are earning extra income on your "growth" investments, you are ready to move to the third level—giving or letting go.

CAN WE EVER BE FINANCIALLY FREE?

We struggle to get a foothold and ease ourselves onto the third step. Through the open doorway we see sunlight filtering through lush green trees giving bloom to beds of roses, geraniums, and impatiens. We hear the sounds of water bubbling over rocks; birds echo sounds of laughter. Freedom is almost ours.

Crash! Steel bars plunge from the ceiling. A bolt snaps. We're locked in. On the bars hangs a metal plate, engraved with these words: "Financial freedom has its price."

THE PRICE OF FREEDOM

In order to escape the prison of our money maze, we must come to terms with what financial freedom really means. Perhaps the best way to define financial freedom is to consider the literal implications of being free. Freedom means emancipation from bondage. Its antonym is enslavement. Financial freedom then, is attained when we are released from the bondage of money and from the hold money has on us.

When money no longer controls our lives, we will have achieved financial freedom. But is that possible? The stone walls and steel bars suggest that it is not.

One of the saddest stories in the Bible is where Jesus tells the rich, young ruler, "Sell everything you have and give it to the poor, and you will have treasure in heaven. Then come, follow me." The young man turned sadly away. The cost of discipleship was too great.

"How hard it is for the rich to enter the kingdom of God!" Jesus then said. "Indeed, it is easier for a camel to go through the eye of a needle than for a rich man to enter the kingdom of God."[1]

And as George MacDonald says, "To have what we want is riches, but to be able to do without is power."

Examples like these cause me to wonder if we should all take a vow of poverty. Unfortunately, being poor doesn't save us from the love of or lust for money and material things. In fact, the love of money has caused greed, slander, murder, and as the Bible says, "all evils," in both the rich and poor alike.[2]

So is the Bible saying that it's sinful to be rich? No. Some of God's most faithful servants were extremely wealthy men. Take Abraham, David, Solomon, and Job, for example.

Job had money in the right perspective. And that perspective is what we need to develop to release the bars and enter the garden of financial freedom.

How did Job feel about money? After God allowed Satan to destroy all that he had, Job remained faithful. "Then Job arose, and rent his robe, and shaved his head, and fell upon the ground, and worshiped. And he said, 'Naked I came from my mother's womb, and naked shall I return; the Lord gave, and the Lord has taken away; blessed be the name of the Lord.' In all this Job did not sin or charge God with wrong."[3]

Job teaches us some important principles. First, all things belong to God. Second, we have nothing unless God gives it to us. This is repeated over and over in the Bible. In Psalms 50:12 God says, " . . . for the world and all that is in it is mine" (RSV).

The third and possibly most important principle is that we are to keep our focus on the Lord and be faithful to him regardless of our circumstances.

Money, whatever the amount, is entrusted to us from God. We are his stewards or agents. We can use it to build ourselves up or to glorify God. We can build up our estates and hoard our treasures, or we can give generously to enhance the Lord's work.

GIVING IS A KEY TO FREEDOM

The more money we have, the more we need to pray for God's special gift of giving. My friend Lauraine told me, "My goal is to out-give God. I know it's impossible." She laughed. "But think how good it will feel to try."

Since God provides us with everything we have, what do we have to lose? As God's agents, we are to put *all* that God gives us to good use. Then he asks that we return only ten percent as a tithe. For many tithing is seen as a burden—one more expense. This, of course, is another of Satan's lies, causing us to see through eyes of greed rather than eyes of giving.

Consider this. If we invested money and handled property for a king, acting as his agent, we would probably earn about ten percent of the profits for our time and talent. Yet when we handle God's resources, he tells us we can keep it all—God gives us one hundred percent. His only stipulation is that we tithe, that we use our funds to facilitate the preaching of the gospel, and that we give generously to those in need.

God has given abundantly. Wouldn't it be wonderful if we could all be free to give ninety percent to God's work and live on ten percent? As I look at my present financial situation that could take a while.

While ninety percent giving may be an unrealistic goal for most of us, perhaps we could set our sights on twenty percent within the next two to five years. This means we must eliminate all outstanding debts, live more simply (meet our needs not wants), live within our means (money left after tithes, savings, and taxes), and invest carefully.

Impossible? For some it may seem so. Yet I have learned recently of Christians in Tanzania whose incomes average $250 a year, yet they tithe twenty percent. I think of the widow who gave up the last of her oil and flour to feed Elisha. And the widow, whose gift pleased Jesus because she gave so much when she had so little.

Freedom to give generously, without feeling strapped, is one key to financial freedom. You hold that key when you affirm and live out these principles:

• I acknowledge God's ownership of all that I have.

• I am a steward of God's property. I want everything I earn and spend to glorify him.

• A tithe is my public acknowledgement of my belief in God as Lord and Master—owner of all.

• I will keep my heart and mind focused on my Lord. He holds eternal treasures. "For where your treasure is, there will your heart be also."[4]

• I consider money as a tool or instrument by which God can achieve his will on earth—and a method by which God meets our needs.

LETTING GO

Freedom from money means being free to be what God wants me to be—no strings attached. No earthly treasures to bind me—that's emancipation. This is the second and final key to releasing the bars and allowing us to enter the garden of financial freedom. Accepting this key and using it to turn the lock is perhaps the most costly act of all.

Could I allow God to cut the chains that bind me to my home, my car, my clothes, my potter's wheel, my typewriter? What if he said, "Sell everything you have and give it to the poor, and you will have treasure in heaven. Then come, follow me," could I? Or would I scramble frantically, trying to relink those chains and make some sort of order out of the chaos in my heart? Could I give up everything?

A woman, Sarah, once came home from a meeting. She pulled into her driveway to find a black, charred, ash-filled foundation that had once been her home. That tragic night, flames had consumed her husband, her children, and all that she had except the clothes she wore.

Sometimes, when I become too attached to a thing or to money, I think of Sarah. I ask myself, *could I accept this loss?* Several years ago I became so involved with my pottery that I spent days and nights in the wonder of creating. One day I felt as if God asked me the question, "Do you love me more than this? Could you give this up for me?"

I cried when I realized how tightly I'd secured the chains. Then I said, "Yes, Lord, but I'll need your help."

God helped me get my passion for pottery under control and led me into another level of service for him—writing. In just that way God can help us overcome a passion for money and what it can buy.

Financial freedom isn't an illusive dream that stands beyond the steel bars of our money maze. Through Bible study, prayer, hard work, and a right relationship with a loving God who shows us the way, we can live in financial freedom. When the heart is right, God removes the barriers and we are free to take the final step out of the money maze into the Garden of Life.

LIFE IN THE GARDEN

Perhaps you're wondering what life is like on the other side of the money maze. It is a place where the glory of God shines with unrestrained abandon, and where we really can count it all joy when trouble comes. Remember the comments about financial freedom in the first part of this chapter? *If only I had enough money, I could . . .*

Life in the Garden means we will not necessarily have riches, but we will have the:

• freedom to invest in people—both time and money for the glory of God.

• freedom to give generously when we are abundantly blessed.

• freedom to receive when we are poor.

• freedom from conceit, pride, and anxiety, regardless of whether we are rich or poor.

• freedom to be content, whatever our situation.

• freedom to give up all of our earthly possessions and to "love the Lord our God with all of our heart, mind and soul and our neighbor as ourselves" (Matt. 22, 37, 39).

• freedom to hear God's voice and respond according to his will.

• freedom to delight in the Lord and receive the abundant fruits he has promised to those who love him.

TIME TO CONSIDER

1. Read Luke 18:18-30. Jesus tells us how difficult it is for the wealthy to enter heaven. Our journey through the money maze gives us a firsthand look at the harsh reality of his words. We, like his disciples, might ask, "Who then can be saved?" What was Jesus' response?

2. Few people successfully find their way through the money maze. As we've seen, it takes considerable time, energy, and commitment. Take a few moments and consider where you are in your money maze. Have you managed to make it through? Are you still caught inside?

3. The tendency for many readers will be to expend some effort to overcome one or two obstacles in their money maze, succumb to pressures, file this book away with the others, and give up. I hope that once you have tasted what financial freedom can mean for you, you will renew your commitment to follow through. If your choice is to continue on, review your goals and achievements. Take time to set new goals and determine specific ways to meet them. Carry on.

4. Sometimes to survive the struggles of life, we need motivation and inspiration. Read Isaiah 40:29-31.

Source Notes

CHAPTER 1

1. Matt. 6:24.
2. 2 Pet. 2:19.
3. Vivian Marino, "Men Still Manage Couples' Finances," *The Oregonian,* 16 April 1990.
4. Venita VanCaspel, *The Power of Money Dynamics* (Reston, VA: Reston Publishing Co., Inc., 1983), p. 2.
5. Prov. 31:10, 25, 26.
6. Deut. 8.
7. Matt. 6:33.
8. Luke 6:38.
9. Luke 19:1-10; 11:37.
10. Matt. 26:6-13.
11. Luke 6:24.
12. Matt. 19:24.
13. Luke 14:33.

14. Richard Foster, *Money, Sex and Power* (San Francisco: Harper & Row Publishers, 1985), p. 22.

CHAPTER 3

1. Luke 16:10-13.
2. Heb. 12:11.

CHAPTER 4

1. Ron Blue, *The Debt Squeeze* (Pomona, CA: Focus On the Family Publishing, 1989), p. 95.
2. Blue, p. 20.
3. Blue, p. 99.

CHAPTER 5

1. Eccles. 3:1.
2. Prov. 20:14 (TLB).
3. Foster, p. 68.

CHAPTER 6

1. Pam Jones and Peggy Young, *Sidetracked Home Executives* (New York: Warner Books, Inc., 1977), p. 10.

CHAPTER 7

1. Luke 14:28, 29 (RSV).
2. Phil. 4:6, 7.

CHAPTER 9

1. James 1:2 (RSV).

CHAPTER 10

1. Luke 18:18-25.
2. 1 Tim. 6:10 (RSV).
3. Job 1:20-22 (RSV).
4. Matt. 6:21 (RSV).

Suggested Reading List

Blue, Ron. *The Debt Squeeze*. Pomona, Calif.: Focus On The Family Publishing, 1989.

Coughran, JoAnne. *Victory at the Supermarket*. Wheaton, Ill.: Tyndale House Publishers, Inc., 1983.

Felton, Sandra. *The Messies Manual: The Procrastinator's Guide to Good Housekeeping*. Old Tappan, N.J.: Fleming H. Revell, 1984.

Fooshee, George and Marjean. *You Can Beat the Money Squeeze*. Old Tappan, N.J.: Fleming H. Revell, 1980.

Foster, Richard J. *Money, Sex and Power*. San Francisco: Harper & Row Publishers, 1985.

Lost in the Money Maze?

Jones, Pam, and Peggy Young. *Sidetracked Home Executives*. N.Y.: Warner Books, Inc., 1977.

MacGregor, Malcolm. *Training Your Children to Handle Money*. Minneapolis: Bethany House, 1980.

MacGregor, Malcolm, and Stanley C. Baldwin. *Your Money Matters*. Minneapolis: Bethany House, 1977.

Proulx, Annie. *What'll You Take for It?* Charlotte, Vt.: Garden Way Publishing Co., 1981.

VanCaspel, Venita. *The Power of Money Dynamics*. Reston, Va.: Reston Publishing Co., 1983.

Wallace, Joanne. *Dress With Style*. Old Tappan, N.J.: Fleming H. Revell, 1983.

Support Groups– Places of Growth and Healing

Women are hungry for teaching and nurturing as they grapple with issues that touch them where they live—loss, self-worth, singleness, remarriage, and numerous other felt needs.

God's heart is to heal and restore his people. In fact, Jesus states this clearly in Luke 4:18, 19 when he announces that God has called him to minister to the oppressed, the hurting, and the brokenhearted. We read throughout the entire New Testament how he wants to equip the Body of Christ to join him in reaching out in love and support of the bruised and wounded. Support groups provide this special place where healing can happen—where women are given time and space to be open about themselves in the context of loving acceptance and honest caring.

WHAT IS A SUPPORT GROUP?

• A support group is a small-group setting which offers women a "safe place." The recommended size is from eight to ten people.

• It is a compassionate, nonthreatening, confidential place where women can be open about their struggles and receive caring and support in a biblically-based, Christ-centered atmosphere.

• It is an accepting place, where women are listened to and loved right where they are.

• It is a place where love and truth are shared and the Holy Spirit is present to bring God's healing.

• It is a place where women learn to take responsibility for making Christ-like choices in their own lives.

• A support group has designated leadership. Coleaders are strongly recommended to share the role of facilitators.

• It is a cohesive and consistent group. This implies "closing" it to additional participants after the second or third meeting before beginning with a new topic and group.

WHAT SUPPORT GROUPS ARE NOT

• They are not counseling groups.

• They are not places to "fix" or change women.

• They are not Bible study or prayer groups as such, although Scripture and prayer are a natural framework for the meetings.

• They are not places where women concentrate on themselves and "stay there." Instead they provide opportunity to grow in self-responsibility and wholeness in Christ.

Small groups often rotate leadership among participants, but because support groups usually meet for a specific time period with a specific mutual issue, it works well for a team of coleaders to be responsible for the meetings. As you can see, leadership is important! Let's take a look at it.

WHAT ARE THE PERSONAL LEADERSHIP QUALIFICATIONS OF A SUPPORT GROUP LEADER?

Courage (1 Cor. 16:13, 14)

A leader shows courage in the following ways as a willingness to:

• She must be open to self-disclosure, admitting her own mistakes and taking the same risks she expects others to take.

• She should lovingly explore areas of struggle with women, and look beyond their behavior to hear what's in their hearts.

• The leader is secure in her own beliefs, sensitive to the Holy Spirit's promptings, and willing to act upon them.

• The leader draws on her own experiences to help her identify with others in the group and be emotionally touched by them.

• She continually examines her own life in the light of God's Word and the Holy Spirit's promptings.

• The leader is direct and honest with members, not using her role to protect herself from interaction with the group.

• A group leader knows that wholeness is the goal and that change is a process.

Willingness to Model (Ps. 139:23, 24)

• A group leader should have had some moderate victory in her own struggles, with adequate healing having taken place. If she is not whole in the area she is leading, she should at least be fully aware of her unhealed areas and not be defensive of them. She should be open to those who can show her if she is misguiding others by ministering out of her own hurt.

• She understands that group leaders lead largely by example, by doing what she expects members to do.

• She is no longer "at war" with her past and can be compassionate to those who may have victimized her. Yet she is a "warrior woman," strong in her resistance of Satan with a desire to see other captives set free.

Presence (Gal. 6:2)

• A group leader needs to either have had personal experience with a support group, or observed enough so she understands how they function.

• A group leader needs to be emotionally present with the group members, being touched by others' pain, struggles, and joys.

• She needs to be in touch with her own feelings so that she can have compassion for and empathy with the other women.

• She must understand that her role is as a facilitator. She is not to be the answer person nor is she responsible for change in others. Yet she must be able to evidence leadership qualities that enable her to gather a group around her.

Goodwill and Caring (Matt. 22:27, 28)

• A group leader needs to express genuine caring, even for those who are not easy to care for. That takes a commitment to love and a sensitivity to the Holy Spirit.

• She should be able to express caring by: (1) inviting women to participate but allowing them to decide how far to go; (2) giving warmth, concern, and support when, and only when, it is genuinely felt; (3) gently confronting a participant when there are obvious discrepancies between

164

her words and her behavior; and (4) encouraging people to be who they are without their masks and shields.

• She will need to be able to maintain focus in the group.

Openness (Eph. 4:15, 16)

• A group leader must be aware of herself, open to others in the group, open to new experiences, and open to life-styles and values that are different from her own.

• As the leader she needs to have an *attitude* of openness, not revealing every aspect of her personal life, but disclosing enough of herself to give participants a sense of who she is.

• A group leader needs to recognize her own weaknesses and not spend energy concealing them from others. A strong sense of awareness allows her to be vulnerable with the group.

Nondefensiveness (1 Pet. 5:5)

• A group leader needs to be secure in her leadership role. When negative feelings are expressed she must be able to explore them in a nondefensive manner.

Stamina (Eph. 6:10)

• A group leader needs physical and emotional stamina and the ability to withstand pressure and remain vitalized until the group sessions end.

• She must be aware of her own energy level, have outside sources of spiritual and emotional nourishment, and have realistic expectations for the group's progress.

Perspective (Prov. 3:5, 6)

• A group leader needs to cultivate a healthy perspective which allows her to enjoy humor and be comfortable with the release of it at appropriate times in a meeting.

Lost in the Money Maze?

• Although she will hear pain and suffering, she must trust the Lord to do the work and not take responsibility for what he alone can do.

• She needs to have a good sense of our human condition and God's love, as well as a good sense of timing that allows her to trust the Holy Spirit to work in the women's lives.

Creativity (Phil. 1:9-11)

• She needs to be flexible and spontaneous, able to discover fresh ways to approach each session.

WHAT SPECIFIC SKILLS DOES A LEADER NEED?

A support group leader needs to be competent and comfortable with basic group communications skills. The following five are essential for healthy and open interaction:

Rephrase

• Paraphrase back to the speaker what you thought she said. Example: "I hear you saying that you felt . . ."

Clarify

• To make sure you heard correctly ask the speaker to explain further. Example: "I'm not hearing exactly what you meant when you said . . ."

Extend

• Encourage the speaker to be more specific. Example: "Can you give us an example . . ."

Ask for Input

• Give the other women opportunity to share their opinions. Example: "Does anyone else have any insight on this?"

Be Personal and Specific

• Use women's names and convey "I" messages instead of "you" messages. "I'm feeling afraid of your reaction, " instead of "You scare me."

ADDITIONAL COMMUNICATION SKILLS

Active Listening

• A good listener learns to "hear" more than the words that are spoken. She absorbs the content, notes the gestures, the body language, the subtle changes in voice or expression, and senses the unspoken underlying messages.

• As a good listener, a leader will need to discern those in the group who need professional counseling and be willing to address this.

Empathy

• This requires sensing the subjective world of the participant—and caring. Of grasping another's experience and at the same time listening objectively.

Respect and Positive Regard

• In giving support, leaders need to draw on the positive assets of the members. Where differences occur, there needs to be open and honest appreciation and acceptance.

• Leaders must be able to maintain confidentiality and instill that emphasis in the group.

Expressing Warmth

• Smiling is especially important in communicating warmth to a group. Other nonverbal expressions are: voice tone, posture, body language, and facial expression.

Genuineness

• Leaders need to be real, to be themselves in relating

with others, to be authentic and spontaneous, to realize that the Holy Spirit works naturally.

WHAT DOES A LEADER ACTUALLY DO?

The leader will need to establish the atmosphere of the support group and show by her style how to relate lovingly and helpfully in the group. She needs to have God's heart for God's people. The following outline specific tasks.

She Organizes Logistics

• The leader helps arrange initial details of the early meetings—time, place, books, etc. (Note: Leaders need to be aware that much secular material, though good in information, is humanistic in application. "I" and "Self" are the primary focus, rather than Christ.)

She Provides Sense of Purpose and Vision

• She reminds the group of their purpose from time to time so that the group remains focused.

She Acts as the Initiator

• She makes sure everyone knows each other, helps them get acquainted and feel comfortable with each other. Makes sure meetings start and end on time.

She Continues as an Encourager to Group Members

• This means basically: encouraging feelings to be expressed, keeping the atmosphere nonjudgmental and accepting, giving feedback, answering questions, clarifying things that were expressed, etc. Praying with and for members.

She Sets Expectations

• She models openness and interest in the group. She

must be willing to take risks by resolving conflicts and clarifying intentions. She holds up standards of confidentiality personally and by reminding the group at each meeting. Confidentiality is crucial to the health of a group, and women should not divulge any private sharing, even to spouses, family, etc.

• She must be watchful and able to guide individuals away from destructive responses. Example: "I have a right to be hurt." She will need to always separate the person from her behavior, meeting the person where she is. Example: "We accept that you are hurt. Do you need to talk about it?"

She Is Sensitive to the Spirit

• She must know when someone needs to be referred to a professional counselor, pastor, etc. and be willing to work that problem through.

• She should be comfortable in ministering freely in the gifts of the Holy Spirit.

She Gives the Guidelines

• It is important that the women know the "ground rules." The leader needs to repeat these often, and *always* when newcomers attend. The following are basic support group guidelines:

1. You have come to give and receive support. No "fixing." We are to listen, support, and be supported by one another, not give advice.

2. Let other members talk. Please let them finish without interruption.

3. Try to step over any fear of sharing in the group. Yet do not monopolize the group's time.

4. Be interested in what someone else shares. Listen with your heart. Never converse privately with someone

while another woman is talking or belittle her beliefs or expressions.

5. Be committed to express your feelings from the heart. Encourage others to do the same. It's all right to feel angry, to laugh, or to cry.

6. Help others own their feelings and take responsibility for change in their lives. Don't jump in with an easy answer or a story on how you conquered their problem or automatically give scripture as a "pat answer." Relate to where they are.

7. Avoid accusing or blaming. Speak in the "I" mode about how something or someone made you feel. Example: "I felt angry when. . . ."

8. Avoid ill-timed humor to lighten emotionally charged times. Let participants work through their sharing even if it is hard.

9. Keep names and sharing of other group members confidential.

10. Because we are all in various stages of growth, please give others permission to be where they are in their growth. This is a "safe place" for all to grow and share their lives.

She Handles Group Discussion

Everyone is different. Your support group will have a variety of personalities. As a leader you will need to protect the group from problem behavior and help the individuals work through it. The following are examples of ways to help each person contribute so that the group benefits:

THEIR BEHAVIOR	YOUR ACTION
Too talkative	Interject by summarizing what the talker is saying. Turn to someone else in the group and redirect a

	question. "Elaine, what do you feel about that?"
A "fixer"	Show appreciation for their help and insight. Then direct a question to someone else. It is important to draw others in so that the woman needing help gets a healthy perspective on her situation and doesn't close off with a quickie solution.
Rambler	Thank them. If necessary, even break in, comment briefly, and move the discussion on.
Antagonist	Recognize legitimate objections when you can. Turn their comments to a constructive view. If all else fails, discuss the attitude privately and ask for their help.
Obstinate	Ask them to clarify. They may honestly not understand what you're talking about. Enlist others to help them see the point. If that doesn't work, tell them you will discuss the matter after the meeting.
Wrong topic	Focus on the subject. Say something like: "Mary, that's interesting, but tonight we're talking about. . . ."

171

Lost in the Money Maze?

Her own problems	Bring it into the discussion if it is related. Otherwise, acknowledge the problem and say: "Yes, I can see why that hurts you. Could we talk about it privately?"
Controversial questions	State clearly what you can or cannot discuss. Say something like: "Problems do exist, but we do not discuss political issues here."
Side conversations	Stop and draw them into your discussion by asking for their ideas.
Personality clash	If a dispute erupts, cut across with a direct question on the topic. Bring others into the discussion: "Let's concentrate on the issue and not make this a personal thing."
Wrong choice of words	Point out that their idea is good and then help them by putting their idea into your words. Protect them from ridicule.
Definitely wrong	Make a clear comment, in an affirming way. "That's another point of view and of course you're entitled to your opinion." Then move on.

Bored	Try to find where their area of interest is. Draw them in to share their experience.
Question you can't answer	Redirect the question to the group. If you don't know the answer, say so and offer to find out.
Never participates	Use direct questions. Remind the group that they will get more out of the meeting when they open up.
Quiet, unsure of self	Affirm them in the eyes of the group. Ask direct questions you are sure they can answer.

She Evaluates the Meeting

• Support groups are a growing experience for everyone, including the leader. Don't be afraid to deal with habitual problems.

• Periodically involve the total group in evaluating how things are going.

She Understands Conflict and Can Handle it Positively

• She understands the biblical pattern for making peace with our sisters in Christ. (See Matthew 5:9 and Romans 14:19.)

• She understands that Jesus has given us clear guidelines to resolve conflict and effect reconciliation and that our motive must be to demonstrate God's love, not vengeance. (See Matthew 5:23, 24 and Matthew 18:15-17.)

• She understands that we approach all situations humbly, knowing that none of us is without sin (Gal. 6:1-4) and that we are seeking reconciliation and forgiveness, not proving who is right and who is wrong.

• She avoids sermonizing.

• She knows that every group will experience conflict on their way to becoming mature and effective, but uses it to help clarify goals and boundaries for the group.

• She defines and describes the conflict as "our group problem."

• She deals with issues rather than personalities.

• She takes one issue at a time.

• She tries to catch issues while they are small rather than letting them escalate over time.

• She invites cooperation, rather than intimidating or giving ultimatums.

• She expresses need for full disclosure of all the facts rather than allowing hidden agendas or leftover hurt feelings.

• She tries to maintain a friendly, trusting attitude.

• She recognizes others' feelings and concerns and opts for a "win-win" feeling or an "us and them" attitude.

• She encourages the expression of as many new ideas and as much new information as possible to broaden the perspective of all involved.

• She involves every woman in the conflict at a common meeting.

• She clarifies whether she is dealing with one conflict or several on-going ones.

She Knows How to Use Feedback

• Feedback helps another person get information on her behavior.

• Feedback is essential in a support group to help the women keep on target and more effectively move through her problems.

174

• She helps make feedback specific. Example: "Just now when we were talking about forgiveness, you changed the subject and started to blame your brother."

• She directs feedback toward behavior that the receiver can do something about. Example: "Would you like to make a choice to release your judgment against your friend?"

• She takes into account the needs of both the receiver and the giver of feedback. It can be destructive if it's given to "straighten out" someone, rather than lovingly point out where that person is.

• She knows feedback is most useful when it is asked for. She can say: "Margaret, are you open to some feedback?"

• She watches for good timing. She tries to give feedback at the earliest opportunity after the given behavior occurs.

• She checks to ensure clear communication. One way of doing this is to have the receiver paraphrase the feedback to see if that is what the sender meant. Example: "I heard you saying that I need to examine my motives for. . . ."

ONE FINAL WORD

Be encouraged, if the Lord has called you to be a support group leader or a member of a group. The Lord promises to do the work of healing, to be with us, to grant us patience, love, mercy—everything we need to follow his commission to love. There will be hard and even painful times. But we can count on him. "He who began a good work in you (in us) will carry it on to completion until the day of Christ Jesus" (Phil. 1:6).

OTHER BOOKS BY AGLOW PUBLICATIONS

Heart Issues

Stanley Baldwin **If I'm Created in God's Image Why Does It Hurt to Look in the Mirror?**
A True View of You

Janet Bly **Friends Forever**
The Art of Lifetime Relationships

Gloria Chisholm **The Gift of Encouragement**
How to be a Warm Shoulder in a Cold World

Michelle Cresse **Beyond Fear**
The Quantum Leap to Courageous Living

Jigsaw Families
Solving the Puzzle of Remarriage

Heather Harpham **Daddy, Where Were You?**
Healing for the Father-deprived Daughter

Diana Kruger **Who Says Winners Never Lose?**
Profiting from Life's Painful Detours

Pam Ravan **Sock Hunting and Other Pursuits of the Working Mother**

Marie Sontag	**When Love is Not Perfect** Discover God's Re-parenting Process

General Books

Barbara Cook	**Love and Its Counterfeits**
Marion Duckworth	**What's Real Anyway?** Eternal Living in an Everyday World
Carol Greenwood	**A Rose for Nana** & Other Touches from an Everyday God
Ranelda Mack Hunsicker	**Secrets** Unlocking the Mystery of Intimacy With God
Kathy Collard Miller	**Healing the Angry Heart** A Strategy for Confident Mothering
	Sure Footing in a Shaky World A Woman's Journey to Security
Quin Sherrer	**How to Pray for Your Children**
Quin Sherrer with Ruthanne Garlock	**How to Forgive Your Children**
Joanne Smith and Judy Biggs	**How to Say Goodbye** Working through Personal Grief

We at Aglow Publications encourage you to stop in at your Christian bookstore and pick up these books. If you do not have access to a Christian bookstore, you may order tollfree at 1-800-755-2456.

Inquiries regarding speaking availability and other correspondence may be directed to Patricia Rushford at the following address:

3600 Edgewood Drive
Vancouver, WA 98661